PUDDINGS

ONE FOR EVERY DAY OF THE YEAR

By

CHARLOTTE POPESCU

Cavalier Paperbacks

© Charlotte Popescu 2007

Line drawings by Roger Phillippo

Published by Cavalier Paperbacks 2007

Cavalier Paperbacks
Burnham House,
Upavon,
Wilts SN9 6DU

www.cavalierpaperbacks.co.uk

ISBN 9781899470242

Printed and bound in Great Britain by Cromwell Press,
White Horse Industrial Park, Trowbridge

CONTENTS

Basic Recipes	5
January	7
February	26
March	45
April	66
May	86
June	105
July	122
August	145
September	164
October	186
November	207
December	228
Index	251

IN PRAISE OF PUDDINGS

In the past and especially between and during the two world wars, puddings were always an important part of the family meal because they filled up young people. They were and still are relatively inexpensive to produce and a home made pudding is on the whole a healthier option for your children than eating crisps, sweets and shop-bought ice creams between meals. Puddings lend themselves to an amazing number of variations and improvisations. They are all here, using ingredients you will probably have in your store cupboard and fruits as they come into season. Rice puddings, batter or steamed puddings are all very economical and when fruits such as apples are in season, or blackberries are abundant in the hedgerows, what better use to put them to than in a crumble, pie or tart.

The recipes are on the whole easy to prepare without too many ingredients. I have three boys myself and, with the amount of puddings they've been trying recently, they have not been leaving the table hungry! If you have a large family and the main course disappears before you have even had time to sit down, then here you will find lots of ideas for puddings to satisfy hungry teenagers. There are also more sophisticated puddings suitable for dinner parties. While researching this book I found many festivals and special days (over 70 in total) and matched them up with puddings to celebrate – I think it adds an extra dimension to the book.

A Frenchman, Monsieur Misson, visiting England in the 1690s wrote: *Blessed be he that invented pudding, for it is a Manna that hits the Palates ... a Manna better than that of the Wilderness, because the people are never weary of it ... to come in Pudding Time is as much as to say, to come in the most lucky moment in the World.*

Charlotte Popescu is the author of several other food related books including **HENS IN THE GARDEN, EGGS IN THE KITCHEN, THE APPLE COOKBOOK** and **FRUITS OF THE HEDGEROW AND UNUSUAL GARDEN FRUITS.**

BASIC RECIPES

Shortcrust pastry
Enough to line a 23cm, 9in or 20cm, 8in flan tin generously
75g, 3oz butter
175g, 6oz plain flour
a little water

Rub the butter into the flour until the mixture resembles breadcrumbs. Add enough cold water to bind the mixture together until you have a smooth dough.

Sweet shortcrust pastry
Enough to line a 23cm, 9in or 20cm, 8in flan tin generously
75g, 3oz butter
175g, 6oz plain flour
1 tbsp caster sugar or icing sugar
1 egg yolk
water

Rub the butter into the flour until the mixture resembles breadcrumbs. Stir in the sugar and bind together with the egg yolk and a little water until you have a smooth dough.

Custard or Crème Anglaise
300ml, ½pt milk
few drops of vanilla essence
25g, 1oz sugar
3 or 4 egg yolks
1 tsp cornflour (optional)

Heat the milk with the vanilla essence and bring just to the boil. Beat the egg yolks with the sugar and cornflour. Pour the milk onto the eggs, whisking as you go. Return to the heat and cook gently until the custard coats the back of the spoon. This should not take long. Do not allow to boil. The cornflour will help the custard thicken but cook on a gentle heat for a couple of minutes longer to get rid of the floury taste.

Meringues

3 egg whites
175g, 6oz caster sugar

Beat the egg whites until really stiff in a clean china or glass bowl. You should be able to turn the bowl upside down without the meringue mixture moving. Whisk in half the sugar and fold in the rest. Spoon onto greased baking sheets and bake in a low oven for 2 - 3 hours.

Whisked Sponge

A whisked sponge is really useful as a base for trifles, summer fruits or other fresh fruits topped with cream. As a variation you can produce a chocolate sponge by substituting 25g, 1oz of the flour with the same amount of cocoa. Whisked sponges also freeze well.

3 eggs
75g, 3oz caster sugar
75g, 3oz plain flour

Whisk the eggs and sugar together until the mixture is thick enough to leave a trail on the surface. Sift the flour and fold into the eggs, being careful not to leave pockets of flour at the bottom of the bowl. Grease a 20cm, 8in cake tin and line with greaseproof paper. Spoon the mixture into the tin and bake in the oven at gas mark 4, 180°C (350°F) for 15 to 20 minutes.

Pancake Batter

300ml, ½pt milk
1 egg
100g, 4 oz plain flour

Whizz all ingredients together in a food processor or put the flour in a bowl, make a well in the centre and gradually beat in the egg and milk until you have a smooth batter.

Cook's Note - Gelatine is a bit tricky now that they are gelatine leaves on sale in supermarkets as well as sachets. The leaves tend to vary in size but on the whole 4 – 6 leaves equals a sachet. A sachet contains about 10g, just a bit less than ½oz of gelatine powder. Remember if you have a **fan oven**, reduce the heat by 20°C.

6

1st January

This day is celebrated in Greece to honour St Basil, the Greek Santa Claus. Children receive gifts and a lucky silver coin is baked into a special sponge cake called vasilopita. The first slice of the cake is set aside for St Basil and the second slice for Christ. The following slices go to members of the family in descending order of age. The cake is flavoured with orange and vanilla. As a variation you could serve it with chocolate sauce.

VASILOPITA - ST BASIL'S CAKE
Serves 6

100g, 4oz butter
175g, 6oz caster sugar
2 eggs
360ml, 12fl oz milk
225g, 8oz plain flour
3 tsp baking powder
grated rind of a small orange
1 tsp vanilla essence

Chocolate fudge sauce (optional)
50g, 2oz plain chocolate
1 tbsp golden syrup
100g, 4oz light brown sugar
1 tbsp cocoa powder
25g, 1oz butter

Cream together the butter and sugar. Beat in the eggs. Sift together the flour and baking powder. Add to the butter mixture alternately with the milk. Add the orange rind and vanilla essence and mix in well. Pour into a greased round 20cm, 8in cake tin. Push a coin into the batter. Bake in the centre of the oven at gas mark 4, 180°C (350°F) for 40 minutes. Cool and turn out the cake. To make the sauce put everything except the butter in a saucepan. Heat gently, bring to the boil and simmer for 5 minutes, while stirring. Beat in the butter. Serve warm with the cake.

2nd January

This is a delicious steamed pudding and very easy to make. It is excellent comfort food for a cold January evening.

STEAMED LEMON SPONGE PUDDING
Serves 4 – 6

2 tbsp lemon curd
100g, 4oz butter
100g, 4oz caster sugar
grated rind of 1 lemon
100g, 4oz self-raising flour
2 large eggs

Spread the lemon curd over the base of a pudding basin. Beat the butter and sugar together and mix in the lemon rind. Gradually add the eggs and the flour. Beat until smooth and spoon over the lemon curd. Cover with greaseproof paper and secure with a rubber band, leaving a pleat so that the pudding has room to rise. Put in a steamer and cook for 1 hour. Turn out the pudding and serve with crème fraîche or some pouring cream.

3rd January

CARAMELISED ORANGES
Serves 4 – 5

4 large oranges
150g, 5oz granulated sugar
150ml, ¼pt water

Peel the oranges, removing all pith and pips. Cut into circles and place in a serving dish. Dissolve the sugar in the water in a small saucepan and then boil until the mixture turns golden. Take it off the heat straightaway and pour over the oranges. It will harden at first but if you put it in the fridge you will find that after a while it dissolves and with the juice from the oranges makes a delicious caramel sauce.

4ᵗʰ January

BLACK TREACLE DELIGHT
Serves 6

3 eggs, separated
100g, 4oz dark brown sugar
225g, 8oz black treacle
300ml, ½pt double cream
2 tbsp brandy

Beat together the egg yolks and sugar until thick and creamy. Add the treacle, warmed slightly. Fold in the double cream and the brandy. Whisk the egg whites until stiff and fold them in. Divide between 6 glasses and leave to chill and set.

5ᵗʰ January

In medieval England *Twelfth Night* was a time for parties and games. Each family would have baked their own Twelfth Night cake with a dried bean and pea inside. Whoever found them would be elected King and Queen of the evening celebrations. The bean was intended for the male, the pea for the female.

TWELFTH NIGHT CAKE
Serves 8 – 10

350g, 12oz butter
225g, 8oz caster sugar
4 eggs
675g, 1½lb plain flour
½ tsp ground allspice
675g, 1½lb mixed dried fruit + 225g, 8oz chopped candied peel
100g, 4oz blanched almonds
3 tbsp brandy + 3 tbsp of sherry

Beat together the butter and sugar, then gradually add the eggs, alternately with the flour. Then add all the other ingredients. Pour into a greased 25cm, 10in cake tin and bake at gas mark 3, 160°C (325°F) for 2 hours.

6ᵗʰ January

This is the twelfth day after Christmas, known as Epiphany, the day the Three Wise Men came to visit baby Jesus. Traditionally housewives would cook an Epiphany Tart and would compete to see who could produce the most differently coloured jams within their tart, separated by lattice; a star design was achieved to celebrate the Epiphany.

EPIPHANY TART
Serves 6 – 8

Shortcrust pastry (see page 5)
spoonfuls of raspberry, strawberry or blackcurrant jams or jellies,
lemon curd or mincemeat - as many different fillings as you want

Roll out the pastry and use to line a greased 23cm, 9in tart tin reserving strips of pastry which you then use to make a lattice design, making compartments for the different jams and jellies you are using. Spoon in the jams and jellies. Bake in the oven at gas mark 4, 180°C (350°F) for 20 to 25 minutes or until the pastry is cooked.

7ᵗʰ January

HOT APPLE MERINGUE TRIFLE
Serves 4 - 6

175g, 6oz sponge fingers
1 tbsp Calvados or brandy + 2 tbsp of water
675g, 1½lb cooking apples, peeled, cored and thinly sliced
25g, 1oz butter
½ tsp ground cinnamon
100g, 4oz brown sugar
3 egg whites
75g, 3oz granulated sugar
75g, 3oz caster sugar

Cover the base of a serving bowl with sponge fingers and pour the Calvados or brandy and water over them. Put the sliced apples in a saucepan and add the butter, cinnamon, brown sugar and a couple of tablespoons of water. Simmer for 15 minutes until the apples are just cooked. Spoon the sliced apples over the sponge fingers. Beat the egg whites gradually adding the granulated sugar. Fold in the caster sugar. Spoon this meringue mixture over the apples. Put in the oven at gas mark 4, 180°C (350°F) for 15 minutes. When the meringue is pale beige it is ready. Serve with cream or crème fraîche. Use the left over egg yolks to make custard to go with tomorrow's Upside Down Pudding.

8ᵗʰ January

PINEAPPLE AND BLUEBERRY
UPSIDE DOWN PUDDING
Serves 4

50g, 2oz butter
50g, 2oz brown sugar
75g, 3oz blueberries
small can of pineapple chunks
100g, 4oz caster sugar
100g, 4oz butter
2 eggs
175g, 6oz self-raising flour
2 tbsp milk

Grease a 20cm, 8in deep cake tin. Cream together the butter and brown sugar and spread over the base of the tin. Arrange the pineapple chunks and blueberries over the top. Beat together all the ingredients for the sponge, adding the milk to give the mixture a dropping consistency. Then spread over the top of the pineapple and blueberries. Bake in the oven at gas mark 4, 180°C (350°F) for about 45 minutes. Turn out so that the pineapple and blueberries are on top and serve with cream or custard.

9ᵗʰ January

RICH CHOCOLATE STEAMED PUDDING
Serves 4 – 6

100g, 4oz plain chocolate
4 tbsp milk
100g, 4oz butter
100g, 4oz dark brown sugar
1 egg, separated
75g, 3oz white breadcrumbs
75g, 3oz self-raising flour

Chocolate fudge sauce (see also page 7)
25g, 1oz plain chocolate
15g, ½oz butter
1 small tin of evaporated milk
50g, 2oz dark brown sugar
2 tbsp golden syrup

Put half the chocolate in a bowl with the milk and heat over a pan of simmering water until the chocolate has melted. Put the butter and sugar in a bowl and beat, gradually adding the melted chocolate and then the egg yolk. Add the breadcrumbs and flour and beat until well mixed. Beat the egg white until stiff and fold it in. Grate the remaining chocolate and fold in. Spoon into a buttered 1.2 litre, 2 pint pudding basin. Cover with greaseproof paper, making a pleat in the centre and secure with a rubber band. Place the basin in the top of a steamer and cover with a lid – steam for 1 hour. To make the chocolate fudge sauce put all the ingredients in a pan and heat gently until melted. Bring to the boil and then lower the heat and simmer for 5 minutes until thick. Turn out the pudding and serve with the sauce.

10th January

A very simple but rather delicious pudding – the brown sugar dissolves into a rich brown syrup.

BROWN SUGAR AND CREAM AMBROSIA
Serves 4

300ml, ½pt double cream
150ml, ¼pt Greek yoghurt
3 tbsp dark brown sugar

Whisk the cream until it thickens and then fold in the yoghurt. Transfer to a serving bowl. Sprinkle two of the tablespoons of sugar over the cream and fold in. Sprinkle the last tablespoon evenly over the top and leave in the fridge for at least a couple of hours before serving.

11th January

VANILLA CUSTARD TART
Serves 6

Sweet shortcrust pastry (see page 5)
4 eggs
150ml, ¼pt single cream
150ml, ¼pt full fat milk
50g, 2oz caster sugar
½ tsp vanilla essence
¼ tsp freshly grated nutmeg

Roll out the pastry and use to line a greased 20cm, 8in flan dish. Chill for 30 minutes and then prick and bake blind in a preheated oven at gas mark 4, 180°C (350°F) for 15 minutes. Meanwhile prepare the custard filling. Whisk the eggs with the cream, milk, sugar and vanilla essence. Pour into the pastry case. Sprinkle nutmeg evenly over the filling. Return to the oven and cook for 20 minutes or until set.

12th January

MANGO MOUSSE
Serves 4 – 6

1 sachet gelatine
juice of 1 lemon
2 ripe mangoes, peeled, stoned and sliced
50g, 2oz caster sugar
150ml, ¼pt double cream
2 egg whites

Sprinkle the gelatine over the lemon juice and leave until spongy, then heat gently until the gelatine has dissolved. Leave to cool. Put the sliced mango and caster sugar in a processor or liquidiser and blend to a purée. Stir in the gelatine and leave until starting to set. Whip the cream and fold it into the purée. Beat the egg whites until stiff and fold them in too. Pour the mixture into a glass bowl or into 6 individual ramekins and chill until set.

13th January

This is the Feast Day of St Hilary and has gained the reputation of being the coldest day of the year. This dates back to 1086 when frost spread over the country and lasted for weeks; it was said to be the severest Arctic spell ever experienced in Britain. So here is a pudding to warm the cockles of your heart.

CHOCOLATE MELTING PUDDINGS
Serves 6

Sauce
75g, 3oz plain chocolate
5 tbsp double cream

For the sponge
150g, 5oz butter, softened
150g, 5oz caster sugar

2 large eggs, beaten
100g, 4oz plain flour
25g, 1oz cocoa powder

To make the sauce to go in the middle, warm the cream in a small saucepan and add the chocolate. Stir until melted and smooth. Cool and then put in the fridge. For the puddings beat together the butter and sugar. Beat in the eggs and gradually stir in the flour sifted with the cocoa powder. Grease six individual mini pudding basins. Put a little sponge into the base of each basin and press it up the sides. Divide the sauce between the six portions. Then top with the remaining sponge mixture to seal in the sauce. Place the puddings on a baking sheet and cook for 15 minutes in the oven at gas mark 4, 180°C (350°F). Turn out and serve with cream or ice cream.

14th January

LEMON TART WITH CHOCOLATE GINGER CRUST
Serves 6 - 8

50g, 2oz butter
1 tbsp golden syrup
75g, 3oz plain chocolate
225g, 8oz ginger biscuits, crushed

Lemon filling
4 eggs
grated rind and juice of 3 lemons
150g, 5oz caster sugar
150ml, ¼pt double cream

Melt the butter, golden syrup and chocolate together and mix in the ginger biscuit crumbs. Use to line a greased 23cm, 9in flan dish, pressing down firmly and chill in the fridge. For the filling beat the eggs and add the lemon rind and juice, sugar and cream. Pour on top of the ginger crust. Bake in the oven at gas mark 4, 180°C (350°F) for about 30 minutes or until the filling is set.

15th January

CHESTNUT CHEESECAKE
Serves 4 - 6

175g, 6oz digestive biscuits, crushed
50g, 2oz butter, melted
225g, 8oz medium fat cream cheese
225g, 8oz sweetened chestnut purée
2 eggs
1 tsp vanilla essence
150ml, ¼pt double cream
50g, 2oz white chocolate

Mix together the digestive biscuit crumbs and butter. Press onto the bottom of a greased 20cm, 8in flan dish. Bake in the oven at gas mark 2, 150°C (300°F) for 10 minutes and then remove and allow to cool. Beat together the cream cheese, chestnut purée, eggs and vanilla essence. Spoon over the biscuit base. Heat the cream and add the white chocolate. Stir until the chocolate melts and then swirl through the chestnut mixture. Chill until you are ready to serve the cheesecake.

16th January

LEMON AND FROMAGE FRAIS MOUSSE
Serves 6

Juice and grated rind of 2 lemons + 1 tbsp water
1 sachet gelatine
3 eggs, separated
175g, 6oz caster sugar
225g, 8oz fromage frais

Mix half the lemon juice with the water and sprinkle the gelatine powder over the liquid, warming it until it dissolves. Beat the egg yolks with the lemon rind, rest of the lemon juice and 75g, 3oz of the caster sugar. Stir the gelatine into the egg yolk mixture. Whisk the egg whites until stiff and whisk in the remaining sugar. Fold the fromage frais into the mousse then fold in the egg whites. Transfer to a serving bowl and chill for a couple of hours.

17ᵗʰ January

Wassailing on this day, which is the Old Twelfth Night, is a custom used in cider-making districts to persuade apple trees to fruit well the following season. Cider is poured onto the roots and shots fired through the branches to ward off evil spirits. Warm cider is drunk and toast soaked in cider is placed in the branches 'for the robin'. Wassailing songs are sung. So why not celebrate with a cider apple cake?

CIDER CAKE
Serves 6 – 8

150ml, ¼pt dry cider
225g, 8oz sultanas
100g, 4oz butter
100g, 4oz light soft brown sugar
2 eggs, beaten
225g, 8oz plain flour
1 tsp bicarbonate of soda

Put the cider and sultanas in a bowl and leave to soak overnight. Cream the butter and sugar together. Gradually beat in the eggs. Add half the flour and the bicarbonate of soda and beat thoroughly. Pour over the sultanas and the cider and mix well. Fold in the remaining flour and pour into a greased 20cm, 8in square cake tin. Bake at gas mark 4, 180°C (350°F) for about 1 hour. Leave to cool in the tin before turning out and cutting into squares.

18th January

Perk yourself up with a Chocolate Fondue.

CHOCOLATE FONDUE
Serves 4 - 6

150ml, ¼pt double cream
175g, 6oz plain chocolate
2 tbsp brandy

Use a selection of fresh fruit such as bananas, kiwi, pineapple, pear and apple slices and strawberries if you can find them. Gently heat the cream and chocolate and stir together until smooth. Add the brandy and keep warm over a low burner. Skewer your pieces of fruit and dip into the chocolate sauce.

19th January

This is the Feast Day of St Canute, King of Denmark, so here is a Danish pudding. This is a quick and easy dish to make and is really tasty. This pudding is also known as 'Peasant Girl with a Veil'.

DANISH APPLE CAKE
Serves 4 – 6

900g, 2lb cooking apples, peeled, cored and sliced
50g, 2oz butter
175g, 6oz brown breadcrumbs
50g, 2oz soft brown sugar
200ml, 7fl oz whipping cream, whipped

Cook the apples in 3-4 tablespoons of water until soft. Beat to a purée. Melt the butter in a frying pan, add the breadcrumbs and sugar and cook until crisp and brown, turning all the time. Turn out onto a plate and leave to cool. Layer the apple purée and breadcrumbs, finishing with a layer of breadcrumbs. Spread the whipped cream over the top and serve.

20th January

CHOCOLATE PECAN TART
Serves 6

Sweet shortcrust pastry (see page 5)
100g, 4oz butter
100g, 4oz golden caster sugar
75g, 3oz plain chocolate
3 eggs
150g, 5oz pecan nuts

Roll out the pastry and line a greased 20cm, 8in flan dish. Bake blind in the oven at gas mark 4, 180°C (350°F) for about 15 minutes. For the filling melt together the butter, sugar and chocolate and stir in the eggs. Spread the pecans over the baked pastry and then pour the chocolate mixture over. Return to the oven for 20 minutes.

21st January

A great winter pudding. This is a suet pudding made in the shape of a roll reminiscent of your school days. The name was made famous by Beatrix Potter's book, *The Tale of Samuel Whiskers* or *The Roly Poly Pudding* in which the stuffing was savoury – Tom Kitten was meant to be the stuffing but luckily he escaped!

JAM ROLY POLY PUDDING
Serves 4

100g, 4oz self-raising flour + 50g, 2oz shredded suet
3 tbsp hot water
8 tbsp strawberry jam

Sift the flour and stir in the suet and enough water to bind the dough together. Knead until smooth. Roll out to an oblong shape and spread half of the jam along the dough. Roll up like a Swiss roll and seal the edges together with a little water. Bake in the oven at gas mark 5, 190°C (375°F) for 40 minutes. Before serving heat the rest of the jam and serve with the jam poured over and custard if liked.

22ⁿᵈ January

CHOCOLATE BAKEWELL TART
Serves 6 – 8

Shortcrust pastry (see page 5)
75g, 3oz blackcurrant jam
50g, 2oz self-raising flour
15g, ½oz cocoa powder
50g, 2oz butter
50g, 2oz caster sugar
1 egg
25g, 1oz ground almonds
½ tsp almond essence

Roll out the pastry and use to line a greased 20cm, 8in flan tin. Spread the jam on the base. Sieve the flour and cocoa. Cream the butter and sugar together and slowly beat in the egg. Fold in the sieved flour and cocoa and stir in the ground almonds and almond essence. Spread the mixture evenly in the pastry case. Roll out the scraps of pastry, cut strips and arrange them in a trellis across the top. Stick the ends onto the flan with a little water. Bake in the oven at gas Mark 4, 180°C (350°F) for a further 15 minutes or until cooked. Serve hot or cold.

23ʳᵈ January

Save the egg yolks for White Chocolate Heavens tomorrow.

PINEAPPLE SORBET
Serves 6 - 8

225g, 8oz granulated sugar
450ml, ¾pt water
1 large pineapple
juice of 1 lemon
2 egg whites

Dissolve the sugar in the water over a gentle heat. Bring to the boil and boil without stirring for 10 minutes. The syrup will have reached the Vaseline stage, feeling oily when rubbed. Leave to cool. Chop up the pineapple, discarding the skin and hard centre. Purée the pineapple flesh and any juice and stir into the cooled syrup with the lemon juice. Pour into a freezer container and half freeze until slushy. Beat the mixture and whisk the egg whites separately, folding them into the pineapple. Return to the freezer and freeze until firm.

24ᵗʰ January

These are little white chocolate ice creams frozen in ramekins. Your children will love them and they are very easy to make.

WHITE CHOCOLATE HEAVENS
Serves 5

75g, 3oz white chocolate
1 tbsp single cream
2 egg yolks
50g, 2oz caster sugar
200ml, 7fl oz double cream

Melt the white chocolate in the microwave or over a pan of simmering water. Stir in the single cream – this will help give a smooth texture. Whisk the egg yolks and sugar together until thick and creamy. Then fold in the melted white chocolate, followed by the double cream. Pour into 5 ramekin dishes and freeze.

25th January

Robert Burns was born on 25th January, 1759. Burns Night is celebrated every year all over Britain by people with Scottish connections and even by those with no Scottish ancestry. This pudding is also known as Cranachan – it traditionally consists of oatmeal, heather honey, cream and whisky. This is a variation with raspberries.

CREAM CROWDIE
Serves 4 - 6

6 heaped tbsp porridge oats
3 tbsp honey
600ml, 1pt double cream
150g, 5oz raspberries
2 tsp caster sugar

Cover a baking tray with greaseproof paper. Preheat the oven to gas mark 3, 160°C (325°F). Mix the honey and oatmeal thoroughly and form into 10 thin round shapes on the baking tray. Cook for 10-20 minutes until golden brown. Allow to cool and they will become wafer-like. Whip the cream and sugar together, add the raspberries and two of the wafers broken up. Gently stir the mixture to create a marble effect. Spoon into a bowl and serve with the rest of the wafers.

26th January

This is Australia Day. Pavlova was invented and named in honour of the Russian ballet dancer Anna Pavlova who toured Australia and New Zealand in the Twenties. Save the egg yolks and use to make the custard for tomorrow's trifle.

PINEAPPLE AND KIWI PAVLOVA
Serves 6 - 8

4 egg whites
225g, 8oz caster sugar

1 tsp cornflour
1 tsp white wine vinegar + 1 tsp vanilla essence
150ml, ¼pt double cream
1 small pineapple, diced or large tin of pineapple chunks, drained
3 kiwi fruit, peeled and sliced

To make the pavlova, beat the egg whites until stiff. Gradually beat in the sugar, a little at a time. Sprinkle the cornflour, vinegar and vanilla over the mixture and fold in carefully. Make a circle with the meringue mixture on a large greased baking sheet. Bake for an hour at gas mark 1, 140°C (275°F). The pavlova should be crisp on the outside with a soft marshmallow centre. Whip the cream and spread over the meringue. Arrange the pineapple and kiwi slices over the cream and serve immediately.

27ᵗʰ January

Why not continue the Burns Night theme with another Scottish pudding?

TYPSY LAIRD - SCOTS TRIFLE
Serves 6 – 8

1 whisked sponge (see page 6)
350g, 12oz raspberry jam
1 wine glass of sherry
2 tbsp Drambuie
300ml, ½pt custard (see page 5)
350g, 12oz raspberries
300ml, ½pt double cream
1 tbsp icing sugar
handful of toasted almonds

Place the sponge in the base of a large glass bowl and spread with the raspberry jam. Mix the sherry and the brandy and sprinkle evenly over the jam and sponge allowing it to soak in. Next add a layer of raspberries and pour the custard over the top. Whip the double cream and icing sugar together and spoon on top of custard. Decorate with toasted almonds.

28th January

MACADAMIA TOFFEE TART
Serves 6

Shortcrust pastry (see page 5)
150g, 5oz macadamia nuts
3 eggs
3 tbsp golden syrup
100g, 4oz butter
100, 4oz dark muscovado sugar
1 tsp vanilla essence

Roll out the pastry and line a greased 20cm, 8in flan dish. Prick and bake blind in the oven at gas mark 4, 180°C (350°F) for 10 minutes. Allow to cool. Scatter the macadamias over the base. Put the eggs, golden syrup, butter, brown sugar and vanilla essence in a bowl and place over a pan of simmering water. Stir, allowing the butter to melt and when evenly combined pour over the nuts. Bake in the oven at gas mark 4, 180°C (350°F) for 25 minutes or until the filling is just set.

29th January

A very simple but unusual pudding – guests may find it difficult to guess what ingredients you've used under the cream.

GINGER BISCUIT PUDDING
Serves 4

200g, 7oz packet ginger biscuits
9 tbsp sherry or a mixture of sherry and water
300ml, ½pt whipped cream

Spread the ginger biscuits out in a small serving dish. Pour the sherry over them and leave to become soft. Stir until smooth. Whip the cream and spread over the ginger base.

30ᵗʰ January

PERSIMMON FOOL
Serves 2

3 persimmons, peeled and sliced
4 tbsp hot water
grated rind of 1 orange and 1 lemon
2 tbsp caster sugar
2 tbsp icing sugar
200ml, 7fl oz double cream, whipped
6 ginger biscuits, crushed

Put the persimmon slices, water, orange peel and caster sugar in a saucepan and cook until soft. Fold the icing sugar and grated lemon peel into the cream. Divide the crushed ginger biscuit crumbs between two glasses. Spoon over the persimmon mixture and top each with cream.

31ˢᵗ January

MOCHA LAYERED CREAMY PUDDING
Serves 4

1 tbsp instant coffee
4 heaped tbsp brown breadcrumbs
2 tbsp drinking chocolate
2 tbsp demerara sugar
150ml, ¼pt double cream
150ml, ¼pt Greek yoghurt

Mix together the coffee, breadcrumbs, drinking chocolate and demerara sugar. Whip the cream and yoghurt together. Layer the cream and breadcrumb mixture in a bowl or 4 individual glasses.

1ˢᵗ February

This is the Celtic Feast of Imbolc – Imbolc means 'in milk' and was traditionally marked as the start of the lactation period of ewes and cows – they would give birth around this time and thus the production of milk would start. Milk was poured onto the earth as part of the ritual. So why not celebrate with a traditional milky rice pudding?

RICE PUDDING
Serves 4 – 6

50g, 2oz pudding rice
600ml, 1pt milk
50g, 2oz light brown sugar
knob of butter

Spoon the rice into a baking dish. Add the milk and sugar and knob of butter. Cook in a slow oven for about 3 hours, stirring every so often. If you like a skin to form, leave without stirring for the last hour.

2ⁿᵈ February

In earlier times Christmas decorations were left up until Candlemas on 2ⁿᵈ February. This festival was established in the 5th century and was traditionally seen by the church as a day of celebrations for the Purification of the Virgin Mary and Presentation of Christ in the Temple. Women who had become mothers or borne children during the previous year were honoured and went to a special service at the church, carrying candles.

This day is also known as The Wives' Feast, so why not celebrate with a good old-fashioned pudding? This pudding has a steamed suet crust, encasing a lemon buttery liquid which oozes out when you cut the crust, and forms a pond around the pudding.

SUSSEX POND PUDDING
Serves 4 - 6

350g, 12oz suet crust pastry
175g, 6oz demerara sugar
100g, 4oz butter
1 large lemon

Grease a 900ml, 1½pt pudding basin with a little butter. Roll out the suet crust pastry to about 2.5cm, 1in thick. Reserve enough for the lid and use the rest to line the basin. Cut the butter into pieces and put some in the basin with half the sugar. Prick the lemon all over with a sharp skewer and press one end into the butter and sugar so that it stands upright. Press the remaining butter and sugar around and over the lemon. Dampen the edge of the crust and fit the remaining suet crust over the top, pressing firmly to seal. Cover with foil and place in a large saucepan half filled with water. Cover the saucepan with a lid and boil gently for 3 hours. Turn out the pudding onto a plate and cut into wedges at the table so that the juices run out.

3rd February

CHESTNUT TRIFLE
Serves 6 – 8

1 whisked sponge (see page 6)
120ml, 4fl oz Madeira
large tin of sweetened chestnut purée
300ml, ½pt double cream, whipped
50g, 2oz plain chocolate, grated

Put the sponge in the bottom of a medium sized serving bowl. Pour Madeira over the sponge. Spread the chestnut purée over the sponge and spoon the cream over the top. Chill in the fridge for at least an hour. Sprinkle the chocolate over the cream just before serving.

4ᵗʰ February

LEMON MERINGUE PIE
Serves 6

Shortcrust pastry (see page 5)
40g, 1½oz cornflour
300ml, ½pt milk
grated rind and juice of 2 lemons
100g, 4oz golden granulated sugar
2 eggs, separated
75g, 3oz caster sugar

Roll out the pastry and use to line a greased 20cm, 8in flan dish. Bake blind in the oven at gas mark 4, 180°C (350°F) for about 15 minutes. To prepare the filling, mix the cornflour with a little milk. Heat the remaining milk and slowly pour it onto the cornflour paste, stirring all the time. Return the mixture to the saucepan and stir in the lemon juice and rind. Bring to the boil and stir to remove any lumps. Simmer for a minute, and then stir in the granulated sugar. Beat in the egg yolks and pour into the flan case. Beat the egg whites until stiff and gradually whisk in half the caster sugar. Fold in the remaining sugar and pile on top of the lemon mixture. Return to the oven for 15 minutes to brown the meringue. Serve with cream.

5ᵗʰ February

PEACHES IN BUTTERSCOTCH SAUCE
Serves 4

50g, 2oz granulated sugar
150ml, ¼pt water
4 peaches, halved with stones removed

Butterscotch Sauce
175g, 6oz brown sugar
25g, 1oz butter

2 tbsp water
150ml, ¼pt single cream
150ml, ¼pt double cream

Dissolve the sugar in the water and add the peach halves. Poach for 10 minutes. Slice the peaches and transfer to a serving bowl. To make the sauce put the sugar, butter and water in a saucepan and heat gently until the sugar dissolves. Then boil until the soft ball stage. Remove from the heat and stir in the single cream. Cool and then stir in the double cream. Pour over the peaches and chill before serving.

6ᵗʰ February

PINEAPPLE CARAMEL CREAM
Serves 6

50g, 2oz granulated sugar
4 tbsp water
300ml, ½pt milk
300ml, ½pt single cream
4 eggs
100g, 4oz caster sugar
small tin of pineapple rings, drained of juice

Put the sugar and water in a saucepan and heat gently until the sugar has dissolved. Bring to the boil and boil until the mixture turns golden brown. Heat the milk and cream and then pour on the caramel, stirring over a gentle heat until the caramel has melted into the milk. Beat the eggs and sugar together until thick. Pour the milk and caramel mixture onto the eggs and sugar and stir to blend together. Purée the pineapple and stir into the caramel cream. Pour into a 1.2 litre, 2 pt soufflé dish, cover with foil and place in a baking tin, half filled with water. Bake at gas mark 3, 160°C (325°F) for about 1 hour or until set. Chill before serving.

7th February

MANGO FOOL WITH BLUEBERRIES
Serves 4 – 6

2 ripe mangoes, peeled and sliced
2 tbsp caster sugar
200ml, 7fl oz crème fraîche
200ml, 7fl oz Greek yoghurt
225g, 8oz blueberries

Purée the mangoes with the caster sugar. Mix together the crème fraîche and yoghurt and fold into the mango purée. Arrange the blueberries in the bottom of a bowl and cover with the mango fool.

8th February

MINI COFFEE CARAMEL PUDDINGS
Serves 6

Coffee caramel
175g, 6oz granulated sugar
4 tbsp water
2 tbsp coffee powder
300ml, ½pt hot water

Sponge
50g, 2oz butter
50g, 2oz caster sugar
1 egg
150g, 5oz self-raising flour

Grease six 150ml, ¼pt pudding basin moulds. To make the coffee caramel, put the sugar and water into a saucepan and, when the sugar has dissolved, cook until a rich brown colour. Mix the coffee with the warm water and pour half onto the caramel. The caramel will splutter so be careful. Stir with a wooden spoon over a gentle heat until the caramel has dissolved. Pour a little into each mould and swirl round the sides. To make the sponge, beat the butter and sugar together, beat in the egg and the flour along with the rest of the coffee liquid. Divide between the six moulds. Bake in the oven at gas mark 4, 180°C (350°F) for 20 minutes. Turn out and serve.

9ᵗʰ February

The Bakewell Pudding was first created in the 1860s at Bakewell's coaching inn. It was the landlady, Mrs Greaves, who usually did the cooking but on this day, when entertaining important guests, the task of making a strawberry tart was left to an inexperienced assistant. The egg and sugar were omitted from the pastry. Then the jam was spread over the pastry and the egg and sugar mixture was put on top and an extra (secret) ingredient was added. It was a great success. This recipe is based on an old recipe allegedly served to Edward VII and Queen Alexandra when they visited Chatsworth House. This filled pastry case is correctly called a pudding, not a tart.

Save the egg whites for tomorrow's Banana and Honey Ice Cream.

BAKEWELL PUDDING
Serves 4 - 6

Shortcrust pastry (see page 5)
2 tbsp raspberry jam
100g, 4oz butter
100g, 4oz caster sugar
2 egg yolks
few drops of almond essence

Line a greased 20cm, 8in flan dish with the pastry. Spread a layer of raspberry jam over the base. Cream together the butter, sugar and egg yolks and beat thoroughly. Put in a bowl over a pan of simmering water and heat until thick. Allow to cool and stir in the almond essence. Spread over the jam and bake in the oven at gas mark 4, 180°C (350°F) for about 25 minutes until lightly browned on top.

10th February

BANANA AND HONEY ICE CREAM
Serves 6

450g, 1lb bananas
150ml, ¼pt double cream
150ml, ¼pt crème fraîche
2 tbsp lemon juice
5 tbsp thick honey
50g, 2oz hazelnuts, roasted and ground
2 egg whites (left over from yesterday)

Mash the bananas and mix in the cream, yoghurt, lemon juice and honey. Pour into a freezer container and freeze, beating twice at hourly intervals. Whisk the egg whites and fold them in after the second beating.

11th February

NORFOLK TREACLE TART
Serves 6

Shortcrust pastry (see page 5)
5 tbsp golden syrup
15g, ½oz butter
1 egg
2 tbsp cream
grated rind of ½ a lemon

Line a greased 20cm, 8in flan dish with the pastry. Warm together the golden syrup and butter. Beat the egg and cream together and pour on the warm syrup. Add the lemon rind. Pour into the pastry case and bake in the oven at gas mark 5, 190°C (375°F) for 20 to 25 minutes.

12ᵗʰ February

ORANGE ICE CREAM
Serves 4 - 6

Grated rind and juice of 2 oranges
6 egg yolks
225g, 8oz caster sugar
300ml, ½pt double cream
2 tbsp Grand Marnier

Whisk the egg yolks with the sugar until very thick. Beat the grated rind and juice from the oranges. Beat the cream and fold it in. Pour into a freezer container and freeze. Make a batch of meringues with left over egg whites.

13ᵗʰ February

It's Shrove Tuesday this month so I have included several pancake recipes. The connection between pancakes and Shrove Tuesday dates back to when fasting in Lent was strictly observed. The pancake ceremonies provided the opportunity to use up the rich foods that were not allowed during Lent, such as butter, eggs and flour.

PANCAKES WITH LEMON AND SUGAR
Makes 8

100g, 4oz plain flour
1 egg
300ml, ½pt milk
sunflower oil for frying
lemon juice and caster sugar for serving

To make the pancakes, process all the ingredients in a food processor or sift the flour into a bowl, make a well in the centre and gradually stir in the egg and milk until you have a smooth batter. Fry the pancakes in a little oil in a frying pan and serve with a squeeze of lemon juice and a sprinkling of sugar.

14ᵗʰ February

A Valentine's celebration feast of puddings for two.

COEURS A LA CREME

225g, 8oz cream cheese
300ml, ½pt double cream
50g, 2oz caster sugar
2 egg whites (save the yolks for the truffles)

Whisk the cream cheese. Whip the cream and fold into the cheese with the sugar. Beat the egg whites and fold them in. Press into two heart shaped moulds and chill until firm. Serve with tropical fruit salad.

TROPICAL FRUIT SALAD

1 ripe mango, peeled and cut into chunks
1 ripe papaya, peeled and cut into chunks
handful of green grapes
1 kiwi fruit, peeled and sliced
1 small can of pineapple chunks, or 3 slices of fresh pineapple
150ml, ¼pt orange juice + 1 tbsp caster sugar
2 bananas, sliced

Put all the fruit except the bananas in a bowl and pour the orange juice over them. Sprinkle with caster sugar and chill. Just before serving add the banana slices.

CHOCOLATE TRUFFLES

175g, 6oz plain chocolate
50g, 2oz unsalted butter
½ tsp vanilla essence
2 egg yolks, beaten
4 tbsp cocoa powder

Melt the chocolate and butter together. Stir in the vanilla essence and egg yolks. Chill to thicken – shape into balls and roll in the cocoa powder.

15ᵗʰ February

BROWN SUGAR MERINGUES
WITH CHESTNUT CREAM
Makes 12 meringues, serves 6 when sandwiched together

3 egg whites (use egg yolks tomorrow)
75g, 3oz caster sugar
75g, 3oz light soft brown sugar
175g, 6oz sweetened chestnut purée
150ml, ¼pt double cream, whipped

Whisk the egg whites until stiff. Mix together the two sugars and while you continue to whisk the egg whites, whisk in a tablespoon of sugar at a time until all is incorporated. The meringue should be very stiff. Put spoonfuls onto greased baking sheets and warm the oven. Cook the meringues for 20 minutes at gas mark 1, 140°C (275°F) and then reduce to gas mark ½, 120°C (250°F) and cook for another 2 hours. Leave in the oven until completely cold. Mix the chestnut purée and cream together and use to sandwich the meringues together.

16ᵗʰ February

COFFEE ALMOND SHORTBREAD TART
Serves 6

225g, 8oz plain four
175g, 6oz butter
100g, 4oz caster sugar
175g, 6oz ground almonds
75g, 3oz caster sugar
75g, 3oz icing sugar
3 egg yolks (from yesterday)
3 tsp coffee essence

To make the shortbread rub the butter into the flour and stir in the caster sugar. Mix to bind together and divide into two, rolling the mixture out into two rounds to fit a 20cm, 8in greased flan tin. Put one round in the base of the dish. To make the filling, mix together the ground almonds, caster sugar and icing sugar. Stir in the egg yolks and coffee essence. Roll out to form another round and press on top of the shortbread. Bake in the oven at gas mark 3, 160°C (325°F) for 40 minutes until golden.

17ᵗʰ February

CREPES SUZETTE
Serves 4

For the crepes
100g, 4oz plain flour
1 egg
1 tbsp oil
300ml, ½pt milk

Juice of 2 oranges
100g, 4oz butter
50g, 2oz caster sugar

1 tbsp Grand Marnier
2 tbsp brandy

Make the pancakes either by mixing all the ingredients in a food processor or sift the flour into a bowl, make a well in the centre and pour in the egg, milk and oil blending everything together until smooth. Cook 8 pancakes and stack with greaseproof paper in between them. To make the orange sauce put the orange juice, butter and sugar into a frying pan and bring to a simmer. Place a pancake into the sauce, fold in half, and half again and then transfer to a warm plate. When all the crepes have been immersed and folded in the sauce, warm the Grand Marnier and brandy in a pan, set alight and then pour over the crepes.

18ᵗʰ February

CHOCOLATE AND BRANDY CHEESECAKE
Serves 6 – 8

225g, 8oz plain chocolate digestives, crushed
50g, 2oz butter, melted
175g, 6oz plain chocolate
2 tbsp brandy
2 eggs, beaten
100g, 4oz brown sugar
350g, 12oz cream cheese
2 tbsp cornflour
icing sugar for dusting

Mix the crushed biscuits and butter together. Spoon into the base of a greased 23cm, 9in flan dish. Press down. Melt the chocolate and stir in the brandy. Beat the eggs and sugar and mix in the cream cheese. Beat until smooth and then stir in the chocolate and cornflour. Pour over the biscuit base and bake in the oven at gas mark 4, 180°C (350°F) for about 25 minutes or until set. Allow to cool and chill for a few hours. Sift with icing sugar and serve.

19th February

Save the egg yolks for tomorrow's Butterscotch Tart.

LEMON MERINGUE ROULADE WITH BLUEBERRIES
Serves 6

4 egg whites
225g, 8oz caster sugar
1 tsp cornflour
1 tsp white wine vinegar
1 tsp vanilla essence
300ml, ½pt double cream
6 tbsp lemon curd
100g, 4oz blueberries
icing sugar

Whisk the egg whites until stiff. Then whisk in the caster sugar a tablespoon at a time. Blend together the cornflour, vinegar and vanilla essence and fold into the meringue mixture. Line a Swiss roll tin with baking parchment and gently spread the meringue mixture out in the tin. Bake in the oven at gas mark 2, 150°C (300°F) for 40 minutes by which time the meringue should be crisp on the outside. Remove from the oven and allow to cool before turning out onto a piece of greaseproof paper. Peel off the lining paper. Whip the cream and mix in the lemon curd. Spread this mixture over the roulade and sprinkle the blueberries over the top. Roll up the roulade from one of the short ends using the paper to help you. Don't worry if the roulade cracks – this is normal. Sprinkle with icing sugar if liked.

20th February
BUTTERSCOTCH TART
Serves 6 - 8

Shortcrust pastry (see page 5)
200g, 7oz dark muscovado sugar
240ml, 8 fl oz single cream

75g, 3oz butter
50g, 2oz cornflour, sifted
4 egg yolks (from yesterday)
1 tsp vanilla essence

Roll out the pastry and use to line a greased 23cm, 9in flan dish. Bake the pastry case blind in the oven at gas mark 5, 190°C (375°F) for 15 minutes. Put the sugar, cream, butter, cornflour, egg yolks and vanilla essence in a bowl and whisk until thick and creamy. Pour into the pastry case. Bake in the oven at gas mark 4, 180°C (350°F) for 20 minutes. Serve warm with crème fraîche or Greek yoghurt.

21st February
COFFEE PANCAKES
WITH CHOCOLATE FUDGE SAUCE
Makes 8 pancakes

100g, 4oz plain flour
1 egg
150ml, ¼pt strong black coffee
150ml, ¼pt single cream

Chocolate Fudge Sauce
75g, 3oz caster sugar
1 tsp vanilla essence
2 tbsp golden syrup
3 tbsp cocoa powder
90ml, 3fl oz boiling water

200ml, 7fl oz cream, whipped

Beat the flour, egg, coffee and cream together until you have a smooth batter. To make the sauce put the sugar, vanilla essence, golden syrup and cocoa powder in a saucepan and pour over the boiling water. Heat gently and when the sugar has dissolved and you have stirred the mixture, boil fast for 5 minutes. It will become fudgy. Fry pancakes in the usual way and serve with chocolate sauce and a dollop of cream if liked.

22ⁿᵈ February

CHOCOLATE SOUFFLÉ
Serves 6 – 8

300ml, ½pt milk
15g, ½oz cornflour
1 tbsp espresso coffee liquid
6 eggs, separated
100g, 4oz caster sugar
225g, 8oz dark chocolate, melted
icing sugar for dusting

Stir a spoonful of the milk into the cornflour and heat the rest with the coffee in a saucepan. Stir the cornflour mixture into the coffee-flavoured milk and keep stirring until the sauce boils. In a bowl whisk the egg yolks with the sugar until thick and beat in the melted chocolate. Stir in the coffee-flavoured milk. Lastly, whisk the egg whites until stiff and fold into the chocolate mixture using a metal spoon. Pour into a greased soufflé dish and bake in the oven at gas mark 6, 200°C (400°F) for 35 minutes. Serve immediately dusted with icing sugar.

23ʳᵈ February

CHESTNUT TIRAMISU
Serves 4 - 6

225g, 8oz mascarpone
100g, 4oz caster sugar
2 eggs, separated
large tin of unsweetened chestnut purée
1 tsp vanilla essence
150ml, ¼pt strong coffee
3 tbsp Marsala
about 20 sponge fingers

1 tbsp grated dark chocolate
2 tsp icing sugar

Beat together the mascarpone, caster sugar and egg yolks. Beat in the chestnut purée and vanilla essence. If the chestnut purée is still lumpy you may have to sieve the mixture. Beat the egg white and fold it into the chestnut mixture. Stir together the coffee and Marsala and dip the sponge fingers in the liquid before laying some in the bottom of a serving bowl. Cover with a layer of the chestnut mixture. Top with the rest of the sponge fingers and finish with a layer of chestnut purée mixture. Chill for a few hours in the fridge. Before serving, sprinkle the grated chocolate over the surface and dust with the icing sugar.

24ᵗʰ February

Save the egg whites for tomorrow's Floating Island.

ZABAGLIONE
Serves 4

4 egg yolks
75g, 3oz caster sugar
120ml, 4fl oz Marsala

Put the egg yolks and sugar in a bowl and beat over a saucepan of simmering water until very pale and thick. Then gradually add the Marsala, a tablespoon at a time while you continue to whisk. You will need to whisk for about 20 minutes. You must add the Marsala slowly and allow the mixture to thicken or it will separate. Pour into 4 glasses and serve.

25th February

If you made yesterday's zabaglione you will have 4 spare egg whites.

FLOATING ISLAND - ILE FLOTTANTE
Serves 4 - 6

4 egg whites
225g, 8oz caster sugar
½ tsp vanilla essence

Crème anglaise
1 egg yolk
2 tbsp caster sugar
2 tbsp plain flour
300ml, ½pt milk
few drops of vanilla essence

Grease a charlotte mould and dust with a little caster sugar. Whisk the egg whites until stiff, add half the caster sugar and continue to whisk until really thick. Fold in the rest of the sugar and vanilla essence. Spoon into the charlotte mould and cover with foil. Place in a roasting tin half filled with water and bake in the oven at gas mark 3, 160°C (325°F) for 30 minutes until the meringue is puffed up and firm. Allow to cool – it will shrink back down. Turn out into a shallow serving bowl. To make the crème anglaise beat together the egg and sugar. Add the flour. Warm the milk and pour over the yolk mixture. Add the vanilla essence. Transfer to a saucepan and heat, stirring constantly, for a couple of minutes until the mixture thickens. Pour the crème anglaise around the meringue.

26th February

BANANA FRITTERS
Serves 4 – 6

150ml, ¼pt milk

1 tbsp oil
1 egg
100g, 4oz plain flour
8 bananas, peeled
2 tbsp caster sugar
oil for frying
icing sugar for dusting

Whizz up the milk, oil, egg and flour in a food processor. Leave to stand for 30 minutes. Meanwhile slice the bananas diagonally and sprinkle with caster sugar. Heat the oil in a deep frying pan and dip each banana slice in the batter before frying until crisp and golden brown. Dust with icing sugar and serve with cream if liked.

27th February

Save the egg yolks you will have left over, after making the meringues, and use to make tomorrow's ice cream.

CHOCOLATE AND WALNUT ICE CREAM CAKE
Serves 6

225g, 8oz plain chocolate
2 tbsp brandy
3 tbsp water
300ml, ½pt double cream
8 medium meringues, crushed (see page 6)
50g, 2oz walnuts, chopped

Melt the chocolate and stir in the brandy and water. Whip the cream and fold into three quarters of the chocolate mixture. Fold in the meringues and walnuts. Pour in the remaining chocolate and swirl to create a marbled effect. Pour into a 20cm, 8in cake tin lined with cling film and freeze for about three hours. Transfer to the fridge about 15 minutes before you want to serve it to soften slightly.

28th February

CHOCOLATE FUDGE ICE CREAM
Serves 4 – 6

4 egg yolks (from yesterday)
1 tbsp cocoa powder
100g, 4oz caster sugar
150ml, ¼pt water
300ml, ½pt double cream, whipped

Fudge
25g, 1oz butter
50g, 2oz plain chocolate
1 tbsp milk
100g, 4oz icing sugar

Beat the egg yolks and cocoa together until thick. Dissolve the sugar in the water and boil rapidly for 5 minutes. Pour the syrup over the egg yolks while continuing to beat until cool and thickened. Fold the whipped cream into the egg yolk mixture. Pour into a freezer container and freeze, beating twice at hourly intervals. To make the fudge put the butter, chocolate and milk in a saucepan over a gentle heat and stir until melted. Pour in the icing sugar and beat to a paste. Chill in the fridge and cut into small pieces. Add to the ice cream when you beat it for the second time. Freeze until firm.

1st March

This is St David's Day in Wales. Celebrate with a Welsh pudding.

WELSH AMBER PUDDING
Serves 6

Shortcrust pastry (see page 5)
2 eggs + 2 egg yolks
50g, 2oz caster sugar
grated rind of ½ a lemon
2 tbsp fine cut marmalade
100g, 4oz butter, melted

Roll out the pastry and line a greased 20cm, 8in flan tin. Prick and bake blind in the oven at gas mark 4, 180°C (350°F) for 10 minutes. Beat together the eggs, egg yolks, sugar, grated lemon rind and marmalade and whisk in the melted butter. Pour into the pastry case and return to the oven for 20 minutes. Serve hot with cream.

2nd March

ORANGE TRIFLE
Serves 4 - 6

1 x 20cm, 8in round sponge cake
4 oranges + juice of 1 orange and grated rind of ½ an orange
1 tbsp Grand Marnier
300ml, ½pt custard (see page 5)
300ml, ½pt double cream
1 tbsp icing sugar

Line the bottom of a serving bowl with slices of the sponge. Peel the oranges and cut into small pieces. Lay on top of the sponge. Mix the juice of 1 orange with the Grand Marnier and pour over the sponge and oranges. Next put a layer of custard over the oranges and then whisk the cream with the icing sugar and grated orange rind and spoon over the custard.

3rd March

TREACLE TART
Serves 6

Shortcrust pastry (see page 5)
75g, 3oz brown breadcrumbs
8 tbsp golden syrup

Roll out the pastry and line a greased 20cm, 8in flan tin. Spread the breadcrumbs over the pastry base and spoon over the golden syrup. Bake in the oven at gas mark 4, 180°C (350°F) for about 20 minutes. Serve hot with single cream.

4th March

This is the feast day of Saint Casimir, Patron Saint of Poland and Lithuania. A traditional cake in Poland would include poppy seeds. Here is a poppy seed cake to celebrate.

POPPY SEED AND LEMON CAKE
Serves 6 - 8

175g, 6oz butter
175g, 6oz caster sugar
finely grated rind of 1 lemon
3 eggs, beaten
175g, 6oz self-raising flour
1 tbsp poppy seeds

For the syrup
75g, 3oz icing sugar
juice of 1 lemon

Beat together the butter and caster sugar. Mix in the lemon rind. Add the eggs gradually with the flour and poppy seeds. Spoon the mixture into a 20cm, 8in greased cake tin and bake in the oven at gas mark 4,

180°C (350°F) for about 25 minutes. Cool the cake slightly. Pierce in several places with a skewer. To make the syrup, dissolve the icing sugar in the lemon juice over a gentle heat. Bring just to boiling point and then pour over the cake. Cover with cling film and leave for about an hour. Serve with cream.

5ᵗʰ March

CRÈME CARAMEL
Serves 4 - 6

175g, 6oz granulated sugar
150ml, ¼pt water
2 egg yolks + 3 eggs (save whites for sorbet on 7 March)
50g, 2oz caster sugar
1 tsp vanilla essence
600ml, 1pt milk

Combine the water and granulated sugar in a saucepan and heat gently until the sugar has dissolved. Bring to the boil and cook without stirring until the mixture is golden brown. Pour into the bottom of a 600ml, 1pt mould or into six individual ramekin dishes. Beat the egg yolks, whole eggs, caster sugar and vanilla essence together. Warm the milk and stir into the egg mixture. Strain and pour onto the sugar syrup. Fill a roasting tin half full with water and place the mould or ramekin dishes in the tin. Bake in the oven at gas mark 3, 160°C (325°F) for 1 hour and 10 minutes (40 minutes if using ramekins) or until set. Cool and then chill for a few hours before serving.

6th March

CHOCOLATE BROWNIE TARTS
Serves 4

Sweet shortcrust pastry (see page 5) use 1 tbsp cocoa powder in
place of 25g, 1oz of the flour
75g, 3oz plain chocolate
50g, 2oz butter
1 egg + 50g, 2oz dark muscovado sugar
½ tbsp self-raising flour

Roll out the pastry and use to line 4 greased tartlet tins. Prick and blake blind for 10 minutes. Melt the chocolate and butter together. Whisk the egg with the sugar. Stir in the chocolate and butter. Sift the flour and fold it in. Divide the mixture between the tartlets and cook in the oven at gas mark 3, 160°C (325°F) for 20 minutes.

7th March

This would go well with yesterday's tartlets if you have any left or with tomorrow's chocolate pudding.

LEMON SORBET
Serves 6 – 8

Peeled rind and juice of 3 lemons
225g, 8oz granulated sugar + 600ml, 1pt water
2 egg whites (saved from 5 March)

Place the lemon rind in a large saucepan with the sugar and water. Dissolve the sugar slowly and then bring to the boil and boil for 10 minutes. Allow the syrup to cool. Add the lemon juice and pour into a freezer container. Freeze until the slushy stage. Beat the egg whites and fold it into the mixture. Return to the freezer and freeze.

8th March

CHOCOLATE MOUSSE CAKE
Serves 6 – 8

3 eggs

48

75g, 3oz caster sugar
150g, 5oz plain chocolate
50g, 2oz butter
1 tsp vanilla essence
25g, 1oz self-raising flour

Whisk the eggs and sugar together until thick. Melt the chocolate and butter together and stir in the vanilla essence. Mix the melted chocolate into the eggs and sugar. Sift the flour and fold it in. Pour into a greased 20cm, 8in cake tin and bake in the oven at gas mark 5, 190°C (375°F) for 25 minutes. Cool before turning out.

9ᵗʰ March

When Lent (the 40 days before Easter) was strictly observed, many cooks thought up new dishes – this recipe, also called Kentish Pudding Pie, is like a baked cheesecake. It was popular around Folkestone.

KENT LENT PIE
Serves 4 – 6

Shortcrust pastry (see page 5)
300ml, ½pt milk
25g, 1oz ground rice
50g, 2oz butter
50g, 2oz caster sugar
2 eggs
finely grated rind of 1 lemon
pinch of grated nutmeg
25g, 1oz currants

Roll out the pastry and use to line a greased 20cm, 8in flan dish. Bake blind in the oven at gas mark 4, 180°C (350°F) for 10 minutes. Meanwhile heat the milk in a saucepan with the ground rice and simmer, stirring until the mixture thickens. Leave to cool. Cream together the butter and sugar. Beat in the eggs, add the lemon rind, nutmeg and the rice mixture. Mix together and pour into the flan case. Sprinkle the currants on top. Return to the oven for 40 minutes. Serve warm.

10ᵗʰ March

CHOCOLATE ROULADE
Serves 6 - 8

175g, 6oz plain chocolate
5 eggs
150g, 5oz caster sugar

Filling
300ml, ½pt double cream
50g, 2oz icing sugar
1 tsp vanilla essence

Melt the chocolate either in a microwave or in a bowl over a pan of simmering water. Whisk the egg yolks with the sugar until thick and pale. Stir in the melted chocolate. Whisk the egg whites until stiff and using a metal spoon fold them into the chocolate mixture until well incorporated. Line a Swiss roll tin with baking parchment and pour the chocolate mixture into the tin, spreading it out evenly. Bake in a pre-heated oven at gas mark 4, 180°C (350°F) for 20 minutes. Then remove from the oven, cover with a damp tea towel and leave for a couple of hours. Use another sheet of baking parchment and sprinkle with icing sugar. Tip the roulade out onto the baking parchment and tear off the bottom piece. Whip the double cream with the icing sugar and vanilla essence and spread over the roulade, before rolling it up like a Swiss roll. Don't worry if it cracks - this is quite normal. Dust with more icing sugar if necessary and serve at once.

11ᵗʰ March

Commonwealth Day is celebrated on the second Monday in March. Why not celebrate with a Carribbean inspired pudding? Guavas are native to the West Indies, have an interesting lemony flavour, are a fantastic source of vitamin C and go well with cream cheese.

GUAVA CHEESECAKE
Serves 6

175g, 6oz digestive biscuits, crushed
50g, 2oz butter, melted
450g, 1lb cream cheese
100g, 4oz caster sugar
2 eggs
1 tsp grated lemon rind + 1 tsp lime juice
1 tsp vanilla essence
1 tin of guavas, drained

Mix the digestive biscuit crumbs into the melted butter and press this mixture onto the base of a greased 20cm, 8in springform cake tin. To make the filling beat the cream cheese with the caster sugar and beat in the eggs. Stir in the grated lemon rind, lime juice and vanilla essence. Pour over the base. Bake the cheesecake in the oven at gas mark 4, 180°C (350°F) for 30 minutes. Leave to cool and then cover with upside down guava halves before serving.

12th March

This Lebanese recipe is said to have been introduced by Lady Hester Stanhope who lived in Lebanon and was the niece of William Pitt the Younger. Lady Stanhope was born on 12 March 1776 and died in 1839.

LADY STANHOPE'S BAALBEK APPLES
Serves 4 - 6

1kg, 2lb eating apples, peeled, cored and quartered
100g, 4oz butter
100g, 4oz caster sugar
1 tsp ground cinnamon

Melt the butter in a frying pan and heat until it turns brown. Add the apple quarters and brown them, turning them once or twice. Remove the apples just before they start to burn. Mix the caster sugar and cinnamon together and sprinkle over the apples. Serve with ice cream if liked.

13th March

CHOCOLATE PANCAKES WITH CREAM
Makes 16 pancakes

75g, 3oz plain flour
25g, 1oz cocoa powder
25g, 1oz caster sugar
2 eggs
200ml, 7fl oz milk
240ml, 8fl oz water
3 tbsp sunflower oil

Filling
300ml, ½pt double cream
1 tbsp icing sugar
extra icing sugar for dusting

Mix all the pancake ingredients together in a blender or food processor. Leave to rest for at least an hour before cooking the pancakes. Whip together the cream and icing sugar and fill each pancake with a dollop of cream. Fold up and dust with icing sugar.

14th March

This is like a light chocolate mousse.

VELVETY CHOCOLATE CREAM
Serves 4 - 6

175g, 6oz full fat cream cheese
50g, 2oz caster sugar
2 eggs, separated
300ml, ½pt double cream
75g, 3oz plain chocolate
25g, 1oz walnuts, crushed
2 tbsp brandy

Beat the cream cheese and sugar together. Beat in the egg yolks. Whip the cream and whisk it into the cream cheese mixture. Melt the chocolate and stir it into the cheese mixture with the walnuts and brandy. Whip the egg whites and fold them in. Pour into a glass bowl or serving dish and chill for at least 2 hours.

15ᵗʰ March

This is an unusual combination of ingredients but delicious all the same. Save the egg yolks to make custard (see page 5) for tomorrow's Spotted Dick.

AVOCADO AND LIME WHIP
Serves 2 – 3

2 ripe avocados
juice of 1 lime
6 tbsp single cream
2 egg whites
50g, 2oz icing sugar, sifted

Purée the avocados with the lime juice and single cream in a food processor. Whisk the egg whites until stiff and whisk in the icing sugar, a little at a time. Carefully fold in the avocado mixture and spoon into individual glasses or into one small serving bowl. Serve straightaway.

16th March

SPOTTED DICK
Serves 4 - 6

275g, 10oz self-raising flour
150g, 5oz shredded suet
50g, 2oz currants
50g, 2oz raisins
75g, 3oz caster sugar
grated rind of 1 lemon
150ml, ¼pt milk

Mix all of the dry ingredients, including the grated lemon rind, together thoroughly. Add enough milk to produce a soft dough. Turn out onto a floured surface. Roll out the mixture to produce a roll approximately 15cm, 6in long and 5cm, 2in in diameter. Lay it on either a tea towel lightly dusted with flour, or sheet of kitchen foil or a double thickness of greaseproof paper, brushed with melted butter. Wrap loosely but securely, leaving enough space for it to rise. Tie or seal the ends. Place in the steamer and cover tightly. Steam for 1½ to 2 hours. Serve cut into thick slices with hot custard.

17th March

This is St Patrick's Day in Ireland.

IRISH COFFEE CHEESECAKE
Serves 4 – 6

175g, 6oz plain chocolate digestive biscuits, crushed
50g, 2oz butter, melted
350g, 12oz cream cheese
100g, 4oz caster sugar
2 eggs
150ml, ¼pt soured cream
2 tbsp Irish whiskey
2 tbsp coffee powder

Mix the crushed biscuits with the butter and press into the base of a greased 20cm, 8in cake tin or flan dish. Chill in the fridge until firm. Mix together the cream cheese, sugar, eggs, soured cream, whiskey and coffee powder. Beat until evenly blended. Pour over the base and bake in the oven at gas mark 4, 180°C (350°F) for 30 minutes or until set.

18ᵗʰ March

It's Mother's Day usually around this time. If you're a Mum with children at home who are old enough to do a bit of cooking, why not give them this recipe to cook for a special treat?

CHOCOLATE SURPRISE PUDDING
Serves 4 – 6

For the sauce
50g, 2oz plain chocolate
100g, 4oz light muscovado sugar
25g, 1oz cocoa powder
1 tsp coffee powder

100g, 4oz plain flour
2 tsp baking powder
25g, 1oz cocoa powder
150g, 5oz light brown sugar
50g, 2oz butter, melted
2 eggs
1 tsp vanilla essence

First put all the ingredients for the sauce in a saucepan with 300ml, ½pt of cold water. Bring slowly to the boil and boil for a couple of minutes, stirring. Leave to cool while you make the sponge. Sift together the flour, baking powder and cocoa powder and stir in the sugar. Add the melted butter, eggs and vanilla. Pour into a greased 20cm, 8in round ovenproof dish. Pour the sauce on top of the sponge mixture. Bake in the oven at gas mark 4, 180°C (350°F) for 30 minutes. As it cooks the sauce will sink down under the sponge, so you will end up with a delicious surprise sauce.

19th March

This is St Joseph's day in Spain, so why not try a Spanish pudding? In Catalonia it is known as Crema Catalana or Crema de Sant Josep and is similar to a crème brulée. The tradition was that the grandmother or maiden aunt living with the family would prepare this pudding on St Joseph's Day and this is still an annual ritual.

CREMA CATALANA
Serves 6 – 8 depending on the size of your ramekin dishes

5 egg yolks (use whites tomorrow)
2 tbsp caster sugar
½ tsp vanilla essence
1 tbsp cornflour
600ml, 1pt cream
225g, 8oz granulated sugar

Beat together egg yolks, caster sugar, vanilla essence and cornflour until thick and smooth. Meanwhile heat the cream until it is just below boiling point. Add to the egg yolk mixture and heat gently until the mixture thickens, stirring constantly. Pour into ramekin dishes and leave to set. Chill in the fridge for at least two hours. To make the caramel topping divide the granulated sugar between the ramekins and place them under a hot grill until the sugar melts. Serve once the caramel has hardened.

20th March

You will have egg whites spare from yesterday's Crema Catalana so use them to make this pavlova.

PAPAYA AND POMEGRANATE PAVLOVA
Serves 6 – 8

4 egg whites
225g, 8oz caster sugar

1 tsp cornflour
1 tsp white wine vinegar
1 tsp vanilla essence
150ml, ¼pt double cream
150ml, ¼pt crème fraîche
2 pomegranates
2 papayas, peeled and sliced

To make the pavlova, beat the egg whites until stiff. Gradually beat in the sugar, a little at a time. Sprinkle the cornflour, vinegar and vanilla over the mixture and fold in carefully. Make a circle with the meringue mixture on a large greased baking sheet. Bake for an hour at gas mark 1, 140°C (275°F). The pavlova should be crisp on the outside with a soft marshmallow centre. Whip the cream with the crème fraîche. Spread this over the pavlova. Halve the pomegranates and remove the seeds and any juice. Discard the skins and pith. Arrange the papaya slices over the pavlova and scatter the pomegranate seeds and juice over the top. Serve at once.

21ˢᵗ March

A simple ice cream but much loved by my children.

MOLASSES ICE CREAM
Serves 4 - 6

3 eggs, separated
75g, 3oz molasses
50g, 2oz icing sugar
300ml, ½pt double cream

Whisk the egg yolks until thick and whisk in the molasses. Whisk the egg whites until stiff and whisk in the icing sugar. Whip the double cream. Fold the cream into the molasses mixture and then fold in the egg whites. Make sure everything is well incorporated and then transfer to a freezer container and freeze until firm.

22ⁿᵈ March

RHUBARB AND APPLE CHARLOTTE
Serves 4

50g, 2oz butter
6 slices white bread, crusts removed
225g, 8oz stewed rhubarb
225g, 8oz stewed apples
¼ tsp ground cinnamon
75g, 3oz caster sugar
2 tbsp sponge cake crumbs

Melt the butter and brush over the slices of bread. Use the bread to coat the sides of a greased 20cm, 8in deep baking dish. Mix the stewed fruit together with the cinnamon and sugar and stir in the cake crumbs. Spoon the fruit over the bread and top with a remaining piece of bread. Bake in the oven at gas mark 4, 180°C (350°F) for about an hour, covering the top with silver foil if it gets too brown. Turn out and serve with cream.

23ʳᵈ March

Sometimes Easter occurs early as is the case in 2008 and so here is a chocolatey recipe.

CHOCOLATE PROFITEROLES WITH COFFEE CREAM AND CHOCOLATE SAUCE
Makes 24

100g, 4oz butter
240ml, 8fl oz water
1 tbsp granulated sugar
150g, 5oz plain flour
2 tbsp cocoa powder
4 eggs

Filling
300ml, ½pt double cream
½ tbsp coffee essence

Chocolate sauce
100g, 4oz plain chocolate + 2 tbsp water
25g, 1oz butter
50g, 2oz icing sugar

To make the profiteroles melt the butter in a pan with the water and sugar. Bring just to the boil and then add the flour, sifted with the cocoa powder, all at once beating until the mixture forms a ball. Cool slightly and then add the eggs a little at a time. Whisk the mixture until smooth and glossy. Put spoonfuls of this choux pastry on dampened baking sheets. Cook in a hot oven for 10 minutes and then lower the heat to gas mark 5, 190°C (375°F) and cook for a further 20 minutes. Transfer to a rack to cool and slit each profiterole. Whip together the double cream and coffee essence and spoon a little into each profiterole. For the chocolate topping put all the ingredients in a bowl over a pan of simmering water. Heat until the chocolate is melted and stir until smooth. Leave to cool and then pile the profiteroles into a pyramid and pour the chocolate sauce over.

24ᵗʰ March
PASSION FRUIT ICE CREAM
Serves 6 – 8

6 passion fruit
3 eggs, separated
100g, 4oz caster sugar
300ml, ½pt double cream, whipped

Cut the passion fruit in half and scoop out the seeds and flesh. Sieve to remove the seeds. Whisk the egg yolks with half the sugar until thick. In another bowl whisk the egg whites until stiff and whisk in the remaining sugar. Fold the fruit purée into the egg yolks, then add the cream and stir until all is well combined. Lastly fold in the egg whites. Turn into a freezer container and freeze until firm.

25th March

MAPLE SYRUP AND PECAN PIE
Serves 6

Sweet shortcrust pastry (see page 5)
150g, 5oz pecans
4 eggs
270ml, 9fl oz maple syrup
100g, 4oz light brown sugar
50g, 2oz butter, melted
1 tsp vanilla essence

Roll out the pastry and use to line a greased 20cm, 8in pie dish. Chill for 30 minutes and then prick and bake blind in the oven at gas mark 4, 180°C (350°F) for 15 minutes. Arrange the pecans over the pastry base. Beat together the eggs, maple syrup, brown sugar, butter and vanilla essence. Pour this mixture over the pecans and return to the oven for 30 minutes. Serve with cream.

26th March

This ice cream has a delicious toffee flavour and no whisking is needed after it goes in the freezer.

BUTTERSCOTCH ICE CREAM
Serves 4 – 6

175g, 6oz granulated sugar
2 tbsp water
150ml, ¼pt evaporated milk
50g, 2oz butter
60ml, 2fl oz double cream
150ml, ¼pt whipping cream
150ml, ¼pt Greek yoghurt

Dissolve the sugar in the water in a small saucepan. Bring to the boil and boil until the sugar turns golden brown. Pour in the evaporated milk but stand back because the mixture will froth up. Stir to combine and then add the butter and double cream. Simmer, stirring for 5 minutes. Allow to cool. Meanwhile whisk the whipping cream and stir in the Greek yoghurt. Fold into the butterscotch mixture and and mix together until smooth. Transfer to a freezer container and freeze until firm.

27ᵗʰ March

PANCAKES WITH SPECIAL LEMON SAUCE
Makes 8 pancakes

Sunflower oil for frying
pancake batter (see page 6)
75g, 3oz butter
225g, 8oz icing sugar
grated rind and juice of 1 lemon
1 egg yolk
icing sugar for dusting

Heat a little oil in a frying pan and cook eight pancakes. Beat the butter and icing sugar together and mix in grated lemon rind and juice. Beat in the egg yolk. Put a spoonful of this sauce on each pancake. Roll up and dust with icing sugar.

28th March

Palm Sunday is the Sunday before Easter (but of course it changes every year). This day commemorates Jesus' last journey to Jerusalem, when people cut palm branches to spread on his path as he rode into the city. In some parts of England it used to be called Fig Sunday because people ate fig pies or puddings on that day.

FIGGY PUDDING
Serves 4 - 6

100g, 4oz butter
2 eggs
175g, 6oz molasses
450g, 1lb cups dried figs, stems removed, chopped
½ tsp grated lemon rind
210ml, 7fl oz buttermilk
50g, 2oz walnuts, chopped
275g, 10oz self-raising flour
½ tsp bicarbonate of soda
½ tsp ground cinnamon
¼ tsp ground nutmeg

Cream the butter until fluffy. Beat in the eggs and molasses. Add the figs, lemon rind, buttermilk, and walnuts and stir together. Sift the flour with the bicarbonate of soda and spices and beat into the mixture. Pour the batter into a greased 900ml, 1½pt soufflé dish. Bake in the oven at gas mark 4, 180°C (350°F) for 1 hour, or until a skewer inserted in the centre comes out clean. Serve with cream.

29ᵗʰ March

The boat race between Oxford and Cambridge is held about this time. This pudding, also known as Burnt Cream, was a speciality of Trinity College, Cambridge.

If you like you can make this with single instead of double cream.

CRÈME BRULÉE
Serves 6

4 egg yolks
50g, 2oz caster sugar
1 tsp vanilla essence
600ml, 1pt double cream
50g, 2oz demerara sugar

Beat the egg yolks with the sugar and beat in the vanilla essence. Heat the cream over a pan of simmering water until just below boiling point. Stir into the egg yolk mixture and strain into 6 greased ramekin dishes. Place the ramekins into a roasting tin half filled with water and bake in the oven at gas mark 4, 180°C (350°F) for about 25 minutes until just set. Leave to cool. Sprinkle demerara sugar over the top of each ramekin and put under the grill to caramelise. Chill for about two hours before serving.

Make a batch of meringues with the left over egg whites.

30ᵗʰ March

Baklava is one of the most famous Middle Eastern pastry puddings, very popular in Greece and Turkey. It is in fact an Armenian sweet (Bahk meaning Lent, halva meaning sweet). Traditionally baklava consists of 40 layers of flaky pastry – one for each day of fasting – it was eaten on Easter Sunday. This recipe uses filo pastry.

BAKLAVA
Serves 6 - 8

175g, 6oz granulated sugar
6 tbsp water
1 tbsp lemon juice
2 tbsp rosewater
100g, 4oz unsalted butter, melted
225g, 8oz filo pastry
100g, 4oz walnuts
1 tbsp light muscovado sugar

First make the syrup by putting the sugar, water and lemon juice in a saucepan and bringing to the boil. Lower the heat and simmer for 10 minutes until syrupy. Add the rosewater and leave to cool. Brush a 30 x 20cm, 12 x 8in baking tin with melted butter. Lay half the sheets in the tin, brushing with butter as you go, folding over the edges if you need to so that the pastry fits into the tin. Sprinkle over the chopped walnuts and the sugar. Continue with the layers of pastry, brushed with butter. Using a sharp knife cut diagonally across the top layer of pastry to make diamond shapes. Bake in the centre of the oven at gas mark 4, 180°C (350°F) for 30 minutes and then for a further hour at gas mark 2, 150°C (300°F). Remove from the oven and pour the cold syrup over the baklava. Cool before cutting up.

31ˢᵗ March

Every year on this day a celebration of an old custom takes place. In the old days the attendants at Clement's Inn used to present each resident with some oranges and lemons and receive a gift in return. The church was decorated with oranges and lemons and the fruit given to the children while the bells played *'Oranges and Lemons, Say the Bells of St Clement's'*.

ST CLEMENT'S MOUSSE
Serves 4 - 6

1 sachet gelatine
grated rind and juice of 2 oranges and 1 lemon
4 eggs, separated
175g, 6oz caster sugar
250ml, 8fl oz whipping cream, whipped

Dissolve the gelatine in a little of the juice from the lemon over a very gentle heat. Whisk the egg yolks and sugar together until pale and thick and whisk in the rest of the lemon juice, orange juice and grated rind. Stir the dissolved gelatine into the egg yolk mixture. Fold in the cream. Lastly whisk the egg whites until stiff and fold in carefully and thoroughly. Spoon into a serving bowl and leave to set.

1st April

It's April Fools' Day. No one is quite sure of its origins. One theory taken from folklore links the day to the town of Gotham in Nottinghamshire. King John had the right to claim any road that he stepped on as public property. When the folk at Gotham heard that King John was coming to their town they refused him entry. The King then sent in his soldiers who arrived to find the town full of lunatics doing crazy things – their foolery was all an act but the King fell for it and declared the town too foolish to be punished. Ever since then April Fools' Day has commemorated their trickery.

MARBLED RHUBARB FOOL
Serves 4

450g, 1lb rhubarb, cut into small chunks
juice of 1 orange
100g, 4oz brown sugar
25g, 1oz butter

Custard
150ml, ¼pt milk
3 egg yolks
1 tsp cornflour

300ml, ½pt double cream, whipped

Put the rhubarb in a saucepan with the orange juice, sugar and butter. Simmer until tender and then pass through a sieve. To make the custard, warm the milk until just below boiling point. Whisk the egg yolks and cornflour together. Pour on the milk and heat gently while stirring. When thickened, strain the custard into a serving bowl and cool before adding the rhubarb purée. Fold in the cream so that streaks run through the rhubarb. Serve immediately. Make some meringues with your left over egg whites.

2nd April

MAPLE SYRUP ICE CREAM
Serves 4 – 6

150ml, ¼pt maple syrup
3 eggs, separated
300ml, ½pt double cream
½ tsp vanilla essence

Heat the maple syrup until just below boiling point. Whisk the egg yolks together and whisk in some of the maple syrup. Stir this back into the hot syrup and cook over a gentle heat until the mixture thickens. Leave to cool. Whip the double cream with the vanilla essence and fold into the maple syrup mixture. Pour into a freezer container and freeze until just becoming firm. Then take out and beat well. Whisk the egg whites until stiff and fold them into the semi-frozen mixture. Freeze again until firm.

3rd April

LEMON AND LIME SOUFFLÉ
Serves 4 – 6

40g, 1½oz butter
40g, 1½oz plain flour
450ml, ¾pt milk
50g, 2oz caster sugar
grated rind of 1 small lemon and 1 lime
juice of ½ a lemon
4 egg whites + 3 egg yolks (use spare egg yolk tomorrow)

Melt the butter in a saucepan and add the flour. Gradually add the milk to make a roux and stir until smooth. Off the heat, stir in the sugar, lemon and lime rind and lemon juice. Beat in the egg yolks. Whisk the egg whites and fold them carefully in using a metal spoon. Turn into a greased 900ml, 1½ pt soufflé dish and bake in a preheated oven at gas mark 5, 190°C (375°F) for about 25 minutes. Serve immediately dusted with icing sugar.

4ᵗʰ April

Paskha means Easter in Russian and is the name of this sweet pudding with dried fruits and almonds traditionally served in Russia. Paskha is eaten after the Orthodox midnight Easter service in which the congregation celebrates the Resurrection of Christ. Many cookbooks call this pudding 'Pashka' incorrectly. For this recipe you need to use a 2 litre, 4 pt new terracotta flowerpot.

Use the egg yolk left over from yesterday's soufflé. You need two more egg yolks - save the egg whites for tomorrow's sorbet.

PASKHA
Serves 6 - 8

150ml, ¼pt double cream
100g, 4oz golden granulated sugar
3 egg yolks
½ tsp vanilla essence
100g, 4oz unsalted butter
675g, 1½lb curd cheese
50g, 2oz raisins
75g, 3oz glace fruits, chopped small
25g 1oz whole candied peel, chopped small
50g, 2oz blanched almonds, toasted and chopped
garnish of small glace fruits, blanched almonds and candied peel

Bring the cream to the boil, then remove from the heat. Beat the sugar and egg yolks until thick before adding to the cream with the vanilla essence. Heat the mixture very gently, stirring until thickened, but don't allow to boil. Remove from the heat and leave to cool. Cream the butter until soft and beat in the cheese. Fold in the cool custard, raisins, chopped fruits and almonds. Line the flowerpot with a double layer of muslin or cheesecloth and pour in the mixture. Cover with a small plate and place a weight on top. Place in the fridge with a bowl underneath to catch the whey. Chill overnight. The next day turn it out onto a serving plate and decorate with the garnish.

5ᵗʰ April

This is refreshing, light and a lovely colour.

KIWI FRUIT SORBET
Serves 6 - 8

350ml, 12 fl oz water
350g, 12oz granulated sugar
juice of 2 lemons
6 large kiwi fruit, peeled
2 egg whites (from yesterday)

Put the water, sugar and juice from 1 lemon in a saucepan and stir over a low heat until the sugar has dissolved. Bring the syrup to the boil and simmer for 3 minutes. Leave to cool. Chop the kiwi fruit and purée in a processor with juice from the other lemon. Add the purée to the cold syrup. Transfer to a freezer container and freeze until the slushy stage. Take out and beat the mixture once. Whisk the egg whites and fold into the half frozen mixture. Return to the freezer and freeze, taking out 15 minutes before you want to serve it, to allow the sorbet to soften.

6ᵗʰ April

CHESTNUT SOUFFLÉ
Serves 6 - 8

4 eggs, separated
1 large tin of sweetened chestnut purée
1 tbsp brandy

Stir the egg yolks into the chestnut purée along with the brandy. Whisk the egg whites together until stiff and gently fold into the chestnut mixture. Transfer to a greased small soufflé dish and cook in the oven at gas mark 6, 200°C (400°F) for 15 minutes. Serve immediately.

7th April

CHOCOLATE CARAMEL TART
Serves 6 - 8

225g, 8oz plain chocolate digestive biscuits, crushed
50g, 2oz butter
100g, 4oz granulated sugar
60ml, 2fl oz water
120ml, 4 fl oz double cream
225g, 8oz plain chocolate
100g, 4oz butter, softened

Melt the butter and mix together with the biscuit crumbs. Press into a greased 20cm, 8in flan dish and bake in the oven at gas mark 4 180°C (350°F) for 10 minutes. Leave to cool. Put the sugar and water in a small saucepan and heat gently until the sugar has dissolved. Then boil until the sugar turns a golden caramel colour. Take off the heat and pour in the cream. The mixture will bubble up. Return to the heat and stir until the caramel dissolves into the cream. Pour onto the chocolate and stir until the chocolate has melted into the caramel and you have a smooth sauce. Add a little water if the mixture thickens too much and then allow to cool a little. Beat in the butter and stir until smooth. Pour onto the chocolate biscuit base and chill until set.

8th April

Traditionally served around Easter, this is a famous dessert from Sicily.

SICILIAN CASSATA
Serves 6 - 8

350g, 12oz sponge cake, thinly sliced
4 tbsp Marsala
450g, 1lb Ricotta cheese
175g, 6oz caster sugar

1 tsp vanilla essence
225g, 8oz candied fruit
75g, 3oz plain chocolate, grated
50g, 2oz pistachio nuts, chopped
75g, 3oz apricot jam + 1 tbsp of water

Line the sides and bottom of a 20cm, 8in mould with greaseproof paper and then line with the sponge cake, reserving some for the lid. Sprinkle with half of the Marsala. Beat together the ricotta, caster sugar and vanilla essence. Stir in the candied fruit, grated chocolate and pistachio nuts. Spoon into the mould and smooth the top. Put the rest of the sponge over the top and sprinkle with the rest of the Marsala. Chill in the fridge overnight. Before serving, turn out onto a serving dish. Warm the apricot jam with a little water, then sieve and use as a glaze by spreading over the cake.

9th April
LEMON CURD AND ALMOND TART
Serves 4 – 6

Shortcrust pastry (see page 5)
3 tbsp lemon curd
50g, 2oz butter
175g, 6oz semolina
175g, 6oz granulated sugar
1 tsp baking powder
1 tsp almond essence
50g, 2oz ground almonds
1 egg, beaten

Roll out the pastry and line a greased 20cm, 8in flan dish. Spread the lemon curd over the base. To make the topping melt the butter in a small saucepan. Remove from the heat and stir in the semolina, sugar, baking powder, almond essence and almonds. Finally stir in the beaten egg. Spread this mixture over the lemon curd. Preheat the oven to gas mark 4, 180°C (350°F) and heat a baking sheet. Place the tart on top of the hot baking sheet and bake for 25 minutes.

10th April

CHAMPAGNE FRUIT SALAD
Serves 4 – 6

100g, 4oz caster sugar
150ml, ¼pt water
2 apples, cored and cut into chunks
2 oranges, peeled, pith removed and sliced
small can of pineapple chunks
2 bananas, sliced
50g, 2oz green grapes, halved
150ml, ¼pt champagne or sparkling cider

Put the sugar and water in a pan and stir over a gentle heat until the sugar dissolves. Set aside. Put the prepared fruit into a bowl. Stir the champagne or cider into the sugar syrup and then spoon over the fruit. Chill before serving.

11th April

BANANAS BAKED IN LEMON SAUCE
Serves 4 – 6

1 egg
100g, 4oz caster sugar
1 tsp cornflour
grated rind and juice of 2 lemons
1 tbsp sherry
6 bananas, peeled
25g, 1oz butter

Whisk the egg and sugar together until thick. Fold in the cornflour, grated rind and juice of the lemons and the sherry. Slice the bananas up and fry them in the butter in a frying pan. Cook for a few minutes and then place them in a baking dish. Cover with the lemon sauce and bake in the oven at gas mark 3, 160°C (325°F) for 20 minutes. Serve hot.

12th April

Although the date for Easter changes every year and can sometimes take place in March it more traditionally occurs in April. And of course you've got to have chocolate at Easter! Make some meringues with the 3 egg whites you will have left over (see page 6).

TRUFFLE TORTE
Serves 6 – 8

1 whisked chocolate sponge (see page 6)
2 tbsp golden syrup dissolved in 90ml, 3fl oz boiling water
225g, 8oz plain chocolate
250ml, 8fl oz double cream
1 tbsp espresso coffee liquid
3 egg yolks
50g, 2oz caster sugar
mini chocolate Easter eggs to decorate

Put the chocolate sponge in a loose-based 20cm, 8in cake tin. Sprinkle with the golden syrup dissolved in the water. Melt the chocolate in the double cream in a bowl set over a pan of simmering water. Stir in the coffee. Whisk the egg yolks and sugar and whisk into the cooled chocolate and cream. Pour over the cake base and smooth the surface. Chill for at least 3 hours or overnight. To serve run a knife around the edge of the torte and carefully remove from the tin. Decorate with mini chocolate eggs.

13th April

GOLDEN SYRUP BREAD PUDDING
Serves 4 - 6

6 tbsp golden syrup
6 slices white bread, crusts removed
50g, 2oz butter
2 eggs
450ml, ¾pt milk

Grease a baking dish (I use an oval dish, 25 x 17.5cm, 10 x 7in) and spoon golden syrup over the base. Butter the slices of bread and cut into fingers. Arrange these butter side up on top of the syrup. Whisk the eggs and milk together and pour on top of the bread. Bake in the oven at gas mark 4, 180°C (350°F) for 40 minutes. Serve straightaway with single cream.

14th April

HONEYCOMB ICE CREAM
Serves 6 – 8

5 tbsp granulated sugar
2 tbsp golden syrup
1 tsp bicarbonate of soda
3 eggs, separated
25g, 1oz caster sugar
450ml, ¾pt double cream
1 tsp vanilla essence

Place the sugar and golden syrup in a small saucepan and heat gently until the sugar melts. Then boil rapidly until the mixture is a golden caramel colour. Take off the heat and sift the bicarbonate of soda over. The mixture will become frothy, stir once and then pour onto a greased baking tin and leave to harden. Cut into small chunks. Beat together the egg yolks and caster sugar until thick. Whip the cream with the vanilla essence until thick and fold into the egg yolk mixture. Whisk the egg whites until stiff and fold them in. Stir the honeycomb chunks gently into the ice cream mixture and spoon into a freezer container. Freeze until firm.

15ᵗʰ April

KIWI FRUIT SYLLABUB
Serves 4

Juice of 1 lemon
4 tbsp sweet sherry
2 tbsp brandy
50g, 2oz caster sugar
300ml, ½pt double cream
3 kiwi fruits

Mix together the lemon juice, sherry, brandy and sugar. Stir until the sugar dissolves. Pour in the cream and whisk until the mixture thickens. Peel and slice the kiwi fruit and mix carefully into the syllabub. Spoon into 4 individual glasses or into a serving bowl.

16th April

This is absolutely delicious and one of our favourite ice creams.

RICH CARAMEL ICE CREAM
Serves 6

175g, 6oz granulated sugar
3 tbsp water
3 tbsp evaporated milk
3 egg yolks (use whites tomorrow)
250ml, 8fl oz double cream, whipped

Dissolve the sugar in a small saucepan with the water. Bring to the boil and boil until a rich golden colour. Turn off the heat and mix in the evaporated milk, standing back as the mixture will froth up. Stir until smooth. Whisk the egg yolks until thick and mix in the caramel plus any fudgy bits that have accumulated. Leave to cool and then fold in the cream. Pour into a freezer container and freeze.

17th April

GRAPE AND HONEY WHIP
Serves 4

1 tbsp caster sugar
grated rind and juice of ½ a lemon
225g, 8oz cream cheese
3 tbsp clear honey
1 tbsp brandy
225g, 8oz seedless green grapes
3 egg whites (from yesterday)

Stir together the sugar, lemon juice, rind, cream cheese, honey and brandy. Chop the grapes and fold them in. Whisk the egg whites and gently fold them in as well. Spoon into serving glasses and chill until ready to serve.

18ᵗʰ April

MARBLED CHOCOLATE CHEESECAKE
Serves 6 – 8

225g, 8oz chocolate chip biscuits, crushed
75g, 3oz butter, melted
100g, 4oz plain chocolate
100g, 4oz butter
175g, 6oz caster sugar
3 eggs
100g, 4oz plain flour
1 tsp vanilla essence
175g, 6oz cream cheese

Stir the biscuit crumbs into the melted butter. Press onto the base of a greased 20cm, 8in flan dish. Melt the chocolate and next lot of butter together. Add half the sugar, two of the eggs and the flour. Mix together and spoon onto the biscuit base. Beat the cream cheese, vanilla essence, rest of the sugar and one remaining egg together and spoon on top of the chocolate mixture. Pull a knife through the two mixtures to swirl them together. Bake in the oven at gas mark 4, 180°C (350°F) for 50 minutes. Serve hot or cold.

19th April

This is Primrose Day so I have devised a Primrose Pudding to celebrate. Primroses are perfectly edible. Disraeli loved primroses and Queen Victoria used to send him bunches from Osborne House and Windsor. Disraeli died on 19 April 1881 and a statue was erected in his honour outside Westminster Abbey. Primroses are placed there on the anniversary of his death each year.

PRIMROSE GATEAU
Serves 4 - 6

3 eggs, separated
100g, 4oz caster sugar
grated rind and juice of 1 lemon
25g, 1oz self-raising flour
25g, 1oz cornflour
3 tbsp mascarpone
3 tbsp lemon curd
handful of primroses

Whisk together the egg yolks and sugar until thick. Stir in the rind and lemon juice. Sift together the flour and cornflour and fold into the egg yolk mixture. Whisk the egg whites in a separae bowl and fold them in until well incorporated. Bake in the oven at gas mark 4, 180°C (350°F) for 20 minutes. Leave to cool slightly before turning out of the tin onto a serving plate. Mix together the mascarpone and lemon curd and spread over the cake. Scatter primroses over the top.

20th April

CHOCOLATE AND LEMON MOUSSE
Serves 6

175g, 6oz white chocolate, cut into chunks
175g, 6oz plain chocolate, cut into chunks
2 eggs, separated

grated rind and juice of 1 lemon
200ml, 7fl oz crème fraîche

Melt the white and dark chocolates in separate bowls in a microwave or over a pan of simmering water. Add one egg yolk to each chocolate mixture, along with the lemon rind and juice and mix half the crème fraîche into each mixture as well. Whisk the egg whites until stiff and fold half into each bowl. Layer the mixtures in a serving bowl or in six glasses and chill before serving.

21ˢᵗ April

This is the Queen's birthday. So why not celebrate with a Queen of Puddings?

QUEEN OF PUDDINGS
Serves 4 - 6

600ml, 1pt milk
pared rind of 1 lemon
25g, 1oz butter
175g, 6oz caster sugar
75g, 3oz fresh white breadcrumbs
3 eggs, separated
4 tbsp blackberry jelly

Heat the milk in a saucepan with the pared lemon rind until the milk is just starting to form a skin. Remove from the heat and stir in the butter and 50g, 2oz of the sugar. Take out the lemon rind and stir until the sugar and butter are melted. Stir in the breadcrumbs and set aside for 30 minutes. Beat the egg yolks into the breadcrumb mixture and pour into a buttered 1 litre, 2 pt ovenproof dish. Put in a roasting tin half filled with water and bake in the oven at gas mark 3, 160°C (325°F) for 45 minutes. Remove from the oven. Spread the blackberry jelly over the surface. Whisk the egg whites and gradually add the remaining sugar. When the meringue is very stiff, spoon it over the jelly and bake in the oven for another 30 minutes until the meringue is golden. Serve with cream.

22nd April

This is Discovery Day in Brazil: Pedro Alvarez Cabral discovered Brazil in 1500. Here is a Brazil nut cake to celebrate.

BRAZIL NUT CAKE WITH CHOCOLATE FILLING
Serves 4 – 6

3 eggs, separated
75g, 3oz caster sugar
25g, 1oz self-raising flour
75g, 3oz Brazil nuts, finely chopped

Filling
100g, 4oz plain chocolate
1 tbsp instant coffee dissolved in a little water
1 egg, separated
120ml, 4 fl oz double cream, whipped

Beat the egg yolks and caster sugar until light. Mix the flour and nuts together and gently fold them into the egg mixture. Beat the egg whites and fold them in. Divide the mixture between two greased 17.5cm, 7in cake tins and bake in the oven at gas mark 4, 180°C (350°F) for 20 minutes. When cooked allow to cool. In the meantime make the chocolate moussey filling. Melt the chocolate, add the coffee and beat in the yolk. Fold in the cream, beat the egg white and fold that in too. Use to fill the cake.

23rd April

St George is the Patron Saint of England. Traditionally George slays a dragon and distributes his reward to the poor. He became very popular because of his chivalrous behaviour and in 1415 he replaced St Edward the Confessor as England's new patron saint and 23rd April was made a national feast day. Here is a sand cake (originally a sandtorte from Austria) topped with a cream cheese mixture and you can make the cross of St George with raspberries.

SAND CAKE WITH RASPBERRIES AND
CREAM CHEESE TOPPING
Serves 6 - 8

200g, 7oz cornflour
25g, 1oz plain flour
225g, 8oz butter
175g, 6oz caster sugar
2 eggs, separated + 1 extra egg white
25g, 1oz ground almonds
grated rind and juice of 1 lemon

For the topping
100g, 4oz cream cheese
50g, 2oz icing sugar
few drops of vanilla essence
a handful of raspberries

Sift together the cornflour and plain flour. Cream the butter and sugar together and beat in the egg yolks, ground almonds and rind and juice of the lemon. Whisk the egg whites until stiff and carefully fold them in. Spoon into a greased 20cm, 8in square cake tin and bake in the oven at gas mark 4, 180°C (350°F) for 40 minutes. Leave to cool. To make the icing beat together the cream cheese, icing sugar and a few drops of vanilla essence. Spread over the cake leaving a gap in the shape of a cross. Place the raspberries in the gap to make the red cross for St George's Day.

24ᵗʰ April

LIME TART
Serves 4 – 6

Sweet shortcrust pastry (see page 5)
3 eggs
75g, 3oz caster sugar
grated rind and juice of 3 limes
90ml, 3fl oz double cream

Roll out the pastry and use to line a greased 20cm, 8in flan dish. Chill for at least 30 minutes before baking blind in the oven at gas mark 5, 190°C (375°F) for 15 minutes. To make the filling whisk the eggs and caster sugar together with the lime rind. Stir in the lime juice followed by the double cream. Pour this mixture into the flan dish and return to the oven for about 30 minutes or until the flan is set. Serve with crème fraîche.

25ᵗʰ April

This is ANZAC day (Australian and New Zealand Army Corps) and commemorates the landing of Australian and New Zealand troops at Gallipoli in 1915. Here is a kiwi fruit pudding to celebrate.

LEMON KIWI SLICES
Makes 14

1 x 500g, 1lb packet puff pastry
25g, 1oz cornflour
50g, 2oz caster sugar
150ml, ¼pt milk
juice of 1 lemon + grated rind of ½ a lemon
1 egg, separated
4 tbsp double cream
6 kiwi fruit, peeled and cut into slices
100g, 4oz icing sugar + 2 tbsp water

Roll out the pastry, cut into 14 small rectangles and place on greased baking sheets. Bake for 15 minutes in the oven at gas mark 7, 220°C (425°F). Cool on a wire rack. Meanwhile mix together the cornflour, sugar and milk and bring to the boil. Stir until the mixture thickens. Add the lemon juice, rind and egg yolk and beat together. Allow to cool and then mix in the cream. Spread a layer of this mixture on the top of each puff pastry slice. Top with two or three slices of kiwi fruit and place the other puff pastry slice on top. Mix together the icing sugar and water and spread this icing on the top of each slice. Allow to set before serving.

26ᵗʰ April

This is a version of the cheese and fruit dessert made at Easter in Russia. Save the egg whites for tomorrow's walnut lemon meringue.

CREAM CHEESE AND PINEAPPLE PASKHA
Serves 6

450g, 1lb cream cheese
100g, 4oz butter
3 egg yolks
100g, 4oz caster sugar
1 tsp vanilla essence
1 small tin of pineapple, drained and crushed or puréed
50g, 2oz flaked almonds, toasted

Beat together the cream cheese, butter and egg yolks. Beat in the caster sugar, fold in the vanilla, pineapple and almonds. Use a small terracotta flowerpot. Line with a double thickness of cheesecloth which has been wrung out in cold water or with muslin. Pour the mixture into the pot. Cover with cling film and put in the fridge overnight. Turn out and serve.

27ᵗʰ April

Use the 3 egg whites from yesterday. Save the 2 extra egg yolks, you will have left over, for tomorrow.

WALNUT LEMON MERINGUE
Serves 6

5 egg whites
225g, 8oz caster sugar
finely grated rind of ½ a lemon + 1 tsp lemon juice
100g, 4oz walnuts, finely chopped
3 tbsp lemon curd
150ml, ¼pt double cream, whipped

Beat the egg whites until stiff and beat in three quarters of the caster sugar. Fold in the rest of the sugar along with the lemon rind, juice and walnuts. Line two 20cm, 8in cake tins with greaseproof paper and divide the meringue mixture between the tins. Bake in the oven at gas mark 1, 140°C (275°F) for 2 hours. Turn the oven off and leave to cool completely. Turn out the two meringue circles and sandwich together with lemon curd mixed with double cream.

28ᵗʰ April
GRANARY BREAD ICE CREAM
Serves 6 - 8

3 tbsp dark brown sugar
25g, 1oz melted butter
75g, 3oz granary breadcrumbs
3 eggs, separated + 2 egg yolks (from yesterday)
1 tbsp honey
1 tbsp brandy
450ml, ¾pt double cream, lightly whipped

Mix the brown sugar with the butter and add the breadcrumbs. Spread this mixture on a baking sheet and bake for 15 minutes turning every so often until the crumbs are toasted. Beat the 5 egg yolks, honey and brandy until thick. Whisk the egg whites and fold into the cream. Then fold this mixture into the egg yolks. Lastly mix in the breadcrumbs. Transfer to a freezer container and freeze until firm but remove from the freezer 15 minutes before you serve it.

29ᵗʰ April

RHUBARB BROWN BETTY
Serves 4

450g, 1lb rhubarb, cut into chunks
100g, 4oz brown sugar
1 tsp ground cinnamon
175g, 6oz breadcrumbs, brown or white
50g, 2oz butter

Put a layer of rhubarb chunks into a greased small ovenproof dish. Mix together the sugar, cinnamon and breadcrumbs and cover the rhubarb with a layer of this mixture. Continue layering until the ingredients are used up. Dot the butter over the top and cook in the oven at gas mark 4, 180°C (350°F) for 40 minutes.

30ᵗʰ April

LEMON AND LIME ICE CREAM
Serves 4 – 6

3 eggs, separated
100g, 4oz caster sugar
grated rind of 1 lemon
grated rind of 1 lime
3 tbsp lime juice
150ml, ¼pt cream, whipped

Whisk the egg yolks and half the sugar until thick and light. Stir in the lemon and lime rinds and lime juice. Fold in the cream. Whisk the egg whites until stiff and whisk in the remaining sugar. Fold into the lemon and lime mixture. Pour the mixture into a container and freeze.

1ˢᵗ May

The Maypole and the choosing of the May Queen took place on 1ˢᵗ May and was always a public holiday so that people could go 'a-Maying' bringing back flowers and branches of trees. The origins can be traced back to ancient times and the goddess Flora and fertility for the coming year. Gold and Silver Cakes were a great favourite of Queen Victoria and this idea is credited to Theodora Fitzgibbon in her book 'A Taste of the West Country'.

GOLD AND SILVER CAKES

For the Silver Cakes
100g, 4oz butter
100g, 4oz caster sugar
175g, 6oz self-raising flour
5 egg whites, beaten stiffly
1 tsp almond essence
2 tbsp ground almonds

Beat the butter and sugar together, add the flour and egg whites in alternate spoonfuls and beat in the almond essence and ground almonds. Spoon into a greased patty tins and bake in the oven at gas mark 4, 180°C (350°F) for 20 minutes.

For the Gold Cakes
Use the same ingredients except use the 5 egg yolks you will have left over and mix in 4 tablespoons of lemon juice, omitting the almond essence and ground almonds. Bake as above. You could serve these piled into a pyramid with chocolate fudge sauce (see page 122).

2ⁿᵈ May

MINT ICE CREAM
Serves 4

100g, 4oz granulated sugar + 150ml, ¼pt water
juice of ½ a lemon

50g, 2oz fresh mint leaves
150g, 5oz mascarpone
3 tbsp Greek style yoghurt

Dissolve the sugar in the water in a small saucepan and boil for 5 minutes. Then add the mint leaves and lemon juice and leave to infuse. Beat the mascarpone and yoghurt together. Strain the syrup and beat into the mascarpone mixture. Transfer to a freezer container and freeze, beating twice at hourly intervals.

3rd May

TOFFEE TART WITH BRAZIL NUT PASTRY
Serves 6

For the pastry
50g, 2oz butter
100g, 4oz plain flour
25g, 1oz Brazil nuts, finely chopped
25g, 1oz icing sugar
1 egg yolk and a little water

75g, 3oz butter
50g, 2oz brown sugar
25g, 1oz plain flour
150ml, ¼pt single cream
3 tbsp golden syrup

Mix together all the ingredients for the pastry in a food processor or rub the butter into the flour and nuts, add the icing sugar and bind together with the egg yolk and water. Bind and shape into a ball. Roll out the pastry and fit into a greased 20cm, 8in flan dish. Prick and bake blind in the oven at gas mark 4, 180°C (350°F) for 15 minutes. Melt the butter and sugar. Stir in the flour. Warm the cream and whisk it into the mixture stirring as it thickens. Off the heat whisk in the golden syrup. Pour into the cooked pastry shell. Chill to set.

4th May

EASY LEMON MOUSSE
Serves 4 – 6

4 eggs, separated
100g, 4oz caster sugar
grated rind and juice of 2 large lemons
1 sachet gelatine
3 tbsp water

Beat the egg yolks in a bowl with the sugar until thick and creamy. Add the lemon juice and rind. Put the gelatine in a small bowl with the water and leave to become spongy. Then put the bowl over a pan of simmering water so that the gelatine dissolves. Cool slightly and stir into the lemon mixture. Leave for a few minutes until it starts to set. Whisk the egg whites until stiff and fold into the lemon mixture. Pour into a serving bowl and leave to set for at least 4 hours.

5th May

MOCHA CREAM CHEESE PIE
Serves 6 - 8

225g,8oz plain chocolate digestive biscuits, crushed
50g, 2oz butter
150g, 5oz plain chocolate
225g, 8oz cream cheese
100g, 4oz caster sugar
1 tsp vanilla essence
2 tsp coffee essence
2 eggs, separated
150ml, ¼pt double cream

Melt the butter and mix together with the biscuit crumbs. Press into a greased 20cm, 8in flan dish and bake in the oven at gas mark 4 180°C (350°F) for 10 minutes. Leave to cool. Melt the chocolate. Beat together the cream cheese, caster sugar, vanilla and coffee essence. Stir in the egg yolks and the melted chocolate. Whip the cream and fold that in too and then whisk the egg whites and fold them in. Spoon into the cooled biscuit base and chill before serving.

6ᵗʰ May

GRAPE AND CREAM CHEESE FLAN
Serves 6 - 8

Shortcrust pastry (see page 5)
225g, 8oz seedless green grapes
75g, 3oz walnuts, chopped
225g, 8oz cream cheese
50g, 2oz caster sugar
300ml, ½pt double cream, whipped
50g, 2oz brown sugar

Roll out the pastry and use to line a greased 20cm, 8in flan tin. Prick and bake blind in the oven at gas mark 4, 180°C (350°F) for 10 minutes. Halve the grapes and lay in the bottom of the cooked flan case with the chopped walnuts. Mix together the cream cheese, sugar and cream and spoon over the grapes. Sprinkle over the brown sugar and caramelise under a hot grill. Then chill before serving.

7ᵗʰ May

RHUBARB CRUMBLE
Serves 4

450g, 1lb rhubarb, cut into chunks
100g, 4oz golden granulated sugar
grated rind of 1 orange
175g, 6oz plain flour
100g, 4oz demerara sugar
50g, 2oz butter

Put the rhubarb in a small baking dish with the sugar and grated orange rind. Make the crumble by rubbing the butter into the flour and stirring in the sugar. Sprinkle over the top of the rhubarb and bake in the oven at gas mark 4, 180°C (350°F) for 30 minutes.

8ᵗʰ May

This is VE day. Why not celebrate with a popular wartime idea? Cabinet Pudding is a classic English dessert usually made with layers of bread, cake or sponge fingers and combined with a dried fruit and custardy filling. It is also sometimes known as Diplomat Pudding.

CABINET PUDDING
Serves 4 – 6

25g, 1oz glace cherries, halved
25g, 1oz angelica, chopped
25g, 1oz caster sugar
450ml, ¾pt milk
3 eggs
few drops of vanilla essence
6 trifle sponges, cut into slices

Put the cherries, angelica and sugar in a bowl and toss to mix. Beat the eggs, milk and vanilla essence and add to the bowl along with the cake slices. Leave to soak for 30 minutes. Turn into a greased pudding basin and cook as for a steamed pudding for an hour.

9ᵗʰ May

LEMON CURD ICE CREAM
Serves 6 – 8

4 eggs, separated
225g, 8oz lemon curd
300ml, ½pt whipping cream, whipped
50g, 2oz icing sugar

Whisk the egg yolks into the lemon curd. Fold into the whipped cream. Whisk the egg whites and whisk in the icing sugar. Fold into the lemon cream until evenly blended. Put into a freezer container and freeze.

10th May

CHERRY SOUFFLÉ OMELETTE
Serves 4

225g, 8oz black cherries, halved and stoned
2 tbsp brandy
1 tbsp icing sugar
4 eggs, separated
2 tsp plain flour
15g, ½oz butter
icing sugar for sprinkling

Marinade the cherries in the brandy and icing sugar for about an hour. Whisk the egg yolks together until light and creamy and whisk the egg whites until stiff. Fold the whites and flour into the egg yolks. Heat the butter in a frying pan and pour in half the egg mixture. Scatter the cherries on top and cover with the remaining egg. Cook for a couple of minutes and then finish off under the grill. Sprinkle with some icing sugar and serve at once.

11th May

WALNUT TREACLE TART
Serves 6

Shortcrust pastry (see page 5)
50g, 2oz walnuts, chopped
6 tbsp golden syrup, warmed
1 tbsp black treacle, warmed
25g, 1oz butter, melted
2 eggs

Roll out the pastry and use to line a greased 20cm, 8in flan tin. Prick and bake blind in the oven at gas mark 4, 180°C (350°F) for 10 minutes. Sprinkle the walnuts over the cooked pastry. Mix together the golden syrup, black treacle, melted butter and eggs and when well combined pour over the walnuts. Return to the oven for 25 minutes.

12ᵗʰ May

MUSCOVADO MERINGUES WITH
PASSION FRUIT AND MASCARPONE
Serves 4 - 6

225g, 8oz light or dark muscovado sugar
4 egg whites (save yolks for tomorrow)
2 passion fruit
100g, 4oz mascarpone
½ tsp vanilla essence

Sieve the muscovado sugar to get rid of any lumps. Whisk the egg whites until very stiff and then whisk in the muscovado sugar a tablespoon at a time, making sure each tablespoon is incorporated before you add the next. Put spoonfuls of meringue onto greased baking sheets and put in the oven at gas mark 1, 140°C (275°F) for 20 minutes, then lower to gas mark ½, 120°C (250°F) and leave for 2 hours. Cut the passion fruit in half, scoop out the seeds and mix with the vanilla essence into the mascarpone. Sandwich the meringues with the mascarpone mixture.

13ᵗʰ May

GIN AND LAVENDER ICE CREAM
Serves 4

5 tbsp gin
1 tbsp dried lavender flowers
4 egg yolks (from yesterday)
175g, 6oz clear honey
300ml, ½pt double cream

Warm the gin a little and pour over the lavender. Leave to infuse for an hour. Strain the gin through a sieve extracting as much gin from the lavender as possible. Beat the egg yolks until thick and creamy and after warming the honey pour over the egg yolks gradually while continuing to whisk. Stir in the flavoured gin. Whip the cream and fold it in. Transfer to a freezer container and freeze until firm.

14th May

CHERRY AND ALMOND TART
Serves 6

Shortcrust pastry (see page 5)
50g, 2oz digestive biscuits, crushed
450g, 1lb black cherries, halved and stoned
50g, 2oz butter
50g, 2oz caster sugar
1 egg
25g, 1oz plain flour
75g, 3oz ground almonds

Roll out two thirds of the pastry and line a greased 20cm, 8in flan dish. Sprinkle the biscuit crumbs over the pastry. Lay the cherries over the crumbs. Cream the butter and sugar, beat in the egg and add the flour and ground almonds. Spread this mixture evenly over the cherries. Use the remaining pastry to make a lattice design over the tart. Brush with milk and bake in the oven at gas mark 6, 200°C (400°F) for about 40 minutes.

15th May

RHUBARB AND BANANA PUDDING
Serves 4 – 6

450g, 1lb rhubarb, cut into chunks
grated rind of ½ a lemon
75g, 3oz granulated sugar
2 tbsp caster sugar
4 bananas, peeled
1 egg white
50g, 2oz flaked almonds

Put the rhubarb into a 20cm, 8in pie dish and sprinkle with lemon rind and sugar. Mash the bananas up with the caster sugar. Beat the egg white until stiff and fold into the banana mixture. Spread on top of the rhubarb to cover completely. Sprinkle the top with the almonds and bake in the oven at gas mark 4, 180°C (350°F) for 30 minutes.

16ᵗʰ May

This is the feast day of St Honorius, Patron Saint of pastry cooks. This cake is a Parisian speciality, named after St Honorius. It combines a shortcrust pastry with choux pastry balls and is also commonly known as Susan or Ball Cake.

GATEAU ST HONORÉ
Serves 6 – 8

Shortcrust pastry (see page 5)

Choux pastry
50g, 2oz plain flour
25g, 1oz butter
1 large egg
few drops of vanilla essence

Caramel syrup
100g, 4oz granulated sugar
4 tbsp water

300ml, ½pt double cream, whipped

Roll out the pastry into a 15cm, 6in circle and place on a greased baking tray. To make the choux pastry, sift the flour. Put the butter and 150ml, ¼pt water in a saucepan and bring to the boil. Remove from the heat and add the flour all at once. Beat until smooth. Leave to cool a little and then beat in the egg and vanilla essence. Place small spoonfuls of the mixture onto greased baking trays and bake in the oven at gas mark 6, 200°C (400°F) for 20 minutes. Cook the pastry circle in the oven at the same time. To make the caramel syrup, dissolve the sugar in two tablespoons of the water and then bring to the boil and boil until caramel coloured. Take off the heat. Stir in the rest of the water and heat again until the caramel dissolves. Dip the choux pastry buns in the caramel syrup and pile around the pastry base, leaving a gap in the middle in which you can spoon the cream.

17th May

EASY CREAMY FLAN
Serves 4 – 6

8 digestive biscuits, crushed
50g, 2oz butter, melted
small tin of condensed milk
150ml, ¼pt double cream
juice of 2 lemons

Mix together the biscuits and melted butter. Press over the base of a greased 17.5cm, 7in flan tin. Put the condensed milk, cream and lemon juice in a bowl and whisk until well combined and thickened. Pour into the flan case and chill for a few hours before serving.

18th May

CHERRY COMPOTE
Serves 4 – 6

1 tbsp redcurrant jelly
50g, 2oz caster sugar
450g, 1lb cherries, halved and stoned
150ml, ¼pt red wine
grated rind and juice of 1 orange

Melt the redcurrant jelly in a frying pan with the sugar. Add the cherries and cook for a few minutes until the juices run. Pour in the wine, orange juice and add the grated rind. Simmer for a couple of minutes. Serve hot or cold.

19ᵗʰ May

PEACH AND WALNUT UPSIDE DOWN PUDDING
Serves 4 – 6

1 tbsp brown sugar
4 peaches, halved and stoned
8 walnut halves
100g, 4oz plain flour + ½ tsp bicarbonate of soda
1 tsp ground ginger + 1 tsp ground cinnamon
100g, 4oz demerara sugar
1 egg
120ml, 4fl oz milk
60ml, 2fl oz sunflower oil

Grease a 23cm, 9in cake tin and sprinkle the brown sugar over the base. Position the peach halves evenly in the tin and put a walnut half in the middle of each one. Sift together the flour, bicarbonate of soda, ginger and cinnamon. Stir in the demerara sugar. Beat together the egg, milk and oil and mix into the dry ingredients. Pour over the peaches and bake in the oven at gas mark 4, 180°C (350°F) for 30 minutes. Invert the pudding onto a plate and serve with crème fraîche.

20ᵗʰ May

RHUBARB YOGHURT ICE
Serves 4 - 6

450g, 1lb rhubarb, cut into chunks
150g, 5oz granulated sugar + 2 tbsp water
150ml, ¼pt ginger wine
210ml, 7fl oz Greek yoghurt
2 egg whites (save yolks for tomorrow)

Put the rhubarb, sugar and water in a saucepan and heat gently, cooking for 10 minutes until the rhubarb is soft. Process to a smooth purée and cool. Stir in the ginger wine. Freeze to the slushy stage and then beat the mixture and stir in the Greek yoghurt. Whisk the egg whites until stiff and fold them in until well blended. Freeze until firm, transferring to the fridge 20 minutes before serving.

Caramelised
Oranges
See page 8

Strawberry Lemon Cheesecake
See page 110

Chestnut
Tiramisu
 See page 40

Sand Cake with Raspberries and Cream Cheese Topping
See page 81

Chocolate Roulade and a slice of Chocolate Roulade
See page 50

Toffee Tart
See page 87

Chocolate Brownie Tart
See page 48

Redcurrant Sorbet
shown here with
meringues
For the sorbet see
page 165
For basic meringues
see page 6

Blackcurrant and Ricotta Dessert See page 122

Treacle Pudding
See page 210

Iced Redcurrant Meringue
See page 139

Poached
Pears and
Strawberries
See page 105

Apple and Blackberry with Shortbread Crumble
See page 184

Chocolate Cream and Raspberry Pudding
See page 130

Apple and
Lemon Curd Tart
See page 234

Pineapple and
Kiwi Pavlova
See page 22

Sticky Toffee
Pudding
See page 250

21ˢᵗ May

CHOCOLATE SYRUP TART
Serves 8

Sweet shortcrust pastry (see page 5)
75g, 3oz butter
100g, 4oz plain chocolate
2 eggs and 2 egg yolks (from yesterday)
3 tbsp golden syrup
175g, 6oz caster sugar
1 tsp vanilla essence

Roll out the pastry and use to line a 23cm, 9cm flan dish. Melt the butter and chocolate together. Beat the eggs and extra egg yolks with the golden syrup, sugar and vanilla essence. Pour into the pastry case. Bake in the oven at gas mark 4, 180°C (350°F) for 30 minutes or until the filling is set – it should remain soft inside. It is best to leave to cool before serving as the mixture will firm up.

22ⁿᵈ May

LEMON SURPRISE PUDDING
Serves 4

15g, ½oz butter
100g, 4oz granulated sugar
2 large eggs, separated
grated rind and juice of a large lemon
1 heaped tbsp plain flour
150ml, ¼pt milk

Beat the butter into the granulated sugar. Beat in the egg yolks, the lemon rind and juice, the flour and milk. Whisk the egg whites and gently fold into the lemon mixture. Spoon into a 20cm x 15cm, 8 x 6in baking tin and place in a roasting tin half-filled with water and bake in the oven at gas mark 4, 180°C (350°F) for 30 minutes. Serve with cream.

23rd May

Dame Nellie Melba was an Australian soprano who performed at Covent Garden Opera House in the 1890s. Escoffier, the famous French chef, was passionately interested in opera and the Majestic Swan which appears in the opera, Lohengrin, gave him the idea of preparing a surprise for the singer. Escoffier had peaches served on a bed of vanilla ice cream, set between two wings of a magnificent swan, shaped out of a block of ice and covered with a layer of icing sugar. He served this with raspberry sauce. Peach Melba was born.

PEACH MELBA
Serves 4

4 peaches
8 small scoops of vanilla ice cream
225g, 8oz raspberries
1 tbsp icing sugar

Simmer the peaches in boiling water, then plunge into cold water to cool them down so that you can peel, halve and remove the stones. If you want to make your vanilla ice cream turn to page 144. Spoon the vanilla ice cream into the dip in each peach half. To make the raspberry sauce, press the raspberries through a sieve, add a few drops of lemon juice and sweeten with icing sugar.

24th May

This is Victoria Day and was celebrated as Queen Victoria's birthday. Manchester Tart, also known as Manchester Pudding or Queen of Puddings Tart, is associated with Queen Victoria. When she made a royal visit to Manchester the then 'everyday local pudding' was made more sophisticated with the addition of a meringue topping. This recipe is adapted from the original Queen Victoria version.

MANCHESTER TART
Serves 6 – 8

Sweet shortcrust pastry (see page 5)
100g, 4oz white breadcrumbs
450ml, ¾pt single cream
150ml, ¼pt milk
3 bay leaves
grated rind of 1 lemon
50g, 2oz caster sugar
4 tbsp brandy
3 egg yolks
4 tbsp strawberry jam

Meringue topping
3 egg whites
175g, 6oz caster sugar

Roll out the pastry and use to line a greased 23cm, 9in flan tin. Prick and bake blind in the oven at gas mark 4, 180°C (350°F) for 10 minutes. Put the breadcrumbs in a saucepan with the cream, milk, bay leaves, lemon rind and caster sugar, stir to mix and simmer for 5 minutes. Remove and discard the bay leaves. Stir in the brandy and beat in the egg yolks. Spread the jam over the pastry base and spoon the breadcrumb mixture over the jam. Return to the oven for 30 minutes. Make the meringue topping by whisking the egg whites until stiff and whisking in the sugar. Spread over the top of the pudding and put back in the oven for 15 minutes.

25ᵗʰ May

LEMON AND LIME SYLLABUB
Serves 3 - 4

Grated rind and juice of 1 lemon
grated rind and juice of 1 lime
50g, 2oz caster sugar
150ml, ¼pt double cream
½ a wine glass of sweet white wine

Mix the juice and rind from the lemon and lime together in a bowl. Add the sugar and stir until dissolved. Add the cream and wine and whisk until thick. Serve in individual glasses or in a small glass bowl.

26ᵗʰ May

TIRAMISU
Serves 6 - 8

6 tbsp brandy
120ml, 4fl oz strong black coffee
20 sponge fingers
450g, 1lb mascarpone
2 eggs, separated
4 tbsp icing sugar
1 tbsp cocoa powder

Mix the brandy and coffee together. Dip the sponge fingers in the liquid and lay in a 20cm, 8in round serving bowl. Pour over any remaining brandy and coffee mixture. Beat together the mascarpone, egg yolks and sugar. Whisk the egg whites and fold them into the mascarpone mixture. Spoon over the sponge fingers. Sprinkle with cocoa powder. Chill for a few hours before serving.

27ᵗʰ May

HAZELNUT ROULADE
Serves 6

5 eggs, separated
150g, 5oz caster sugar
75g, 3oz hazelnuts, roasted and ground
2 tbsp golden syrup
300ml, ½pt whipping cream
1 tbsp instant coffee, dissolved in 2 tbsp hot water
1 tbsp icing sugar plus extra for sprinkling

Line a Swiss roll tin with greaseproof paper. Put the egg yolks and caster sugar into a bowl and whisk until thick. Fold in the ground hazelnuts. Whisk the egg whites until stiff and continue to whisk while you drizzle in the golden syrup. Fold into the egg yolk mixture. When thoroughly combined pour into the tin and tilt to even out the mixture. Bake in the oven at gas mark 4, 180°C (350°F) for 15 minutes. Remove from the oven and cover with a layer of greaseproof paper and then with a damp tea towel. Leave for a few hours. Whip the cream and whisk in the coffee and icing sugar. Place a piece of greaseproof paper on your work surface and cover with icing sugar. Tip the roulade out onto the icing sugar. Carefully peel off the lining paper. Spread the cream mixture over the roulade and roll up. Sprinkle with icing sugar and serve.

28th May

LEMON FUDGE TART
Serves 6 – 8

Sweet shortcrust pastry (see page 5)
5 eggs
grated rind and juice of 4 lemons
275g, 10oz caster sugar
150g, 5oz butter

Roll out the pastry and use to line a greased 23cm, 9in flan dish. Prick and bake blind in the oven for 15 minutes at gas mark 4, 180°C (350°F). Meanwhile melt the butter. Whisk the eggs, sugar, lemon juice and grated rind and whisk in the melted butter. Pour over the pastry base while it is still warm. Return to the oven and cook for 25 minutes at gas mark 4, 180°C (350°F). Serve warm.

29th May

This is Oak Apple Day in commemoration of Charles II's escape from the Roundheads. It was traditional to enjoy a plum pudding, washed down with beer – especially at the Royal Hospital in Chelsea which was founded by Charles II on 29th May 1682.

PLUM PUDDING
Serves 4 – 6

100g, 4oz plain flour
100g, 4oz white breadcrumbs
1 eating apple, peeled and grated
75g, 3oz granulated sugar
75g, 3oz shredded suet
100g, 4oz currants
½ tsp mixed spice
2 tbsp black treacle
210ml, 7fl oz milk

Mix the flour and breadcrumbs together in a bowl, then add the apple, sugar, suet, currants and spice. Warm the treacle and mix into the milk. Pour onto the other ingredients and stir together. Spoon into a greased pudding basin, cover with greaseproof paper and steam for approximately 3 hours.

30ᵗʰ May

GOOSEBERRY AND ELDERFLOWER FOOL
Serves 4 - 6

450g, 1lb gooseberries
2 tbsp water
2 heads of elderflowers
100g, 4oz caster sugar
1 egg white
300ml, ½pt double cream

Place the gooseberries in a saucepan with the water and elderflowers. Bring to the boil and simmer for about 10 minutes until soft. Then stir in the sugar. Sieve the fruit and allow the purée to cool. Whip up the egg white and cream in separate bowls and fold them both into the gooseberry purée. Spoon into a seving bowl and chill before serving.

31ˢᵗ May

A retro recipe here – something that was popular in the sixties and seventies but first appeared at the beginning of the 20ᵗʰ Century. Originating in America, the Devil's Food Cake, was probably thus named because it was so rich it was immoral to eat it! Although this could be served at tea time it makes a luxuriously indulgent pudding served with cream.

DEVIL'S FOOD CAKE WITH LUXURY
CHOCOLATE FUDGE ICING
Serves 8

100g, 4 oz plain chocolate + 150ml, ¼pt water
100g, 4oz butter
225g, 8oz light brown sugar
2 eggs
225g, 8oz self-raising flour
150ml, ¼pt soured cream

For the icing
150ml, ¼pt single cream
50g, 2oz plain chocolate
100g, 4oz light brown sugar
50g, 2oz butter, cut into pieces
¼ tsp vanilla essence

Melt the chocolate with the water and stir until smooth. Cream the butter and sugar together. Add the eggs one at a time and beat. Blend in the chocolate. Sift the flour and beat it in alternately with the soured cream. Divide the mixture between two greased 23cm, 9in cake tins and bake in the oven at gas mark 4, 180°C (350°F) for 25 minutes. Turn out and cool. To make the icing put the cream, chocolate and sugar into a small saucepan and melt over a low heat then bring to the boil and cook, stirring until the mixture thickens and a small amount dropped into cold water forms a soft ball. Add the butter and vanilla essence and beat until thick. Sandwich the two cakes together with half the icing and spread the rest on top.

1ˢᵗ June

ELDERFLOWER FRITTERS
Makes 10 fritters

100g, 4oz plain flour
2 small eggs
300ml, ½pt milk
10 elderflower heads
caster sugar and lemon for serving
sunflower oil for deep frying

Make up the batter by whizzing together the flour, eggs and milk in a food processor. Wash and trim the elderflower heads leaving the stalk so that you can dip each one in the batter. Heat the oil in a frying pan, dip the elderflower heads in the batter and fry them, using the stalk to remove each one when it is golden brown. Trim off the stalks and serve with caster sugar and lemon.

2ⁿᵈ June

Pears and strawberries work well together and this is a light, healthy pudding – English strawberries should just be coming into season.

POACHED PEARS WITH STRAWBERRIES
Serves 4

300ml, ½pt water
100g, 4oz granulated sugar
1 tsp vanilla essence
4 pears, peeled, halved and cored
25g, 1oz pine nuts
225g, 8oz strawberries, hulled and sliced

Boil the sugar and water for a few minutes. Add the vanilla essence and poach the pears in this syrup until they are just tender. Turn over every so often. Put them in a serving dish and stick the pine nuts into the sides of the pears. Boil the syrup to reduce by half. Add the strawberries and allow to simmer for two minutes. Spoon over the pears.

3rd June

GOOSEBERRY CHEESECAKE
Serves 8

175g, 6oz digestive biscuits, crushed
50g, 2oz butter, melted
225g, 8oz gooseberries + 1 tbsp water
100g, 4oz caster sugar
350g, 12oz cream cheese
2 eggs, separated
300ml, ½pt double cream
1 sachet gelatine

Stir the biscuit crumbs into the melted butter. Use this biscuit mixture to line the base of a greased 20cm, 8in tin. Cook the gooseberries in a pan with the water and sugar until soft. Then purée and sieve them to remove the pips. Mix together the cream cheese and egg yolks and stir in the gooseberry purée. Whip the cream and fold it in. Dissolve the gelatine in a little water and stir into the mixture. Whisk the egg whites until stiff and fold them in. Pour the cheesecake mixture onto the biscuit base and transfer to the fridge to set.

4th June

Eton Mess is a famous dish from Berkshire. When the annual prize-giving is held at Eton College, parents and pupils have a picnic on the playing fields. Among the dishes served is this mixture of strawberries, cream and crushed meringues, to which the school has lent its name. According to Robin Weir in *'Recipes From The Dairy'*, Eton Mess was served in the 1930s in the school's sock (tuck) shop, and was originally made with either strawberries or bananas mixed with ice cream or cream. Meringue was a later addition.

ETON MESS
Serves 4 – 6

450g, 1lb strawberries, hulled and sliced

300ml, ½pt double cream
6 meringues

Put the strawberries in a large serving bowl. Whip the double cream. Crush the meringues. Fold the cream and meringues into the strawberries and serve.

5ᵗʰ June

LEMON AND ELDERFLOWER SYLLABUB
Serves 2 – 3

300ml, ½pt double cream
2 tbsp elderflower cordial
1 tbsp lemon juice

Whip the cream and gently fold in the elderflower cordial and lemon juice. Serve chilled in glasses.

6ᵗʰ June

Sticky and sweet, this is one for the children.

STICKY CARAMEL TART
Serves 6

Sweet shortcrust pastry (see page 5)
75g, 3oz butter
225g, 8oz demerara sugar
small tin of evaporated milk
2 tbsp golden syrup

Roll out the pastry and line a greased 20cm, 8in flan tin. Prick and bake blind for 15 minutes in the oven at gas mark 4, 180°C (350°F). To make the filling put all the ingredients in a saucepan and heat gently until the demerara sugar has dissolved and the butter has melted. Continue to cook for 5 minutes – the mixture will thicken. Pour into the pastry case and chill.

7ᵗʰ June

STRAWBERRY CREAM ICE
Serves 4 – 6

100g, 4oz caster sugar
150ml, ¼pt water
450g, 1lb strawberries, puréed
300ml, ½pt double cream
2 tsp vanilla essence

Dissolve the sugar in the water and simmer until syrupy which will take about 5 minutes. Allow to cool. Mix the strawberry purée with the sugar syrup. Whip the cream until it is thick and then fold into the strawberry mixture. Stir in the vanilla essence and pour the mixture into a freezer container. Freeze until firm but remove from the freezer about 30 minutes before you want to serve it.

8ᵗʰ June

PINEAPPLE FRANGIPANE TART
Serves 6 – 8

Sweet shortcrust pastry (see page 5)
225g, 8oz fresh or canned pineapple, drained and cut into chunks

Topping
100g, 4oz butter
100g, 4oz caster sugar
2 eggs
100g, 4oz Brazil nuts, ground

Roll out the pastry and use to line a greased 20cm, 8in flan case. Place the pineapple pieces over the pastry base. For the topping cream together the sugar and butter. Beat in the eggs and ground nuts. Spread over the pineapple. Bake in the oven at gas mark 4, 180°C (350°F) for 30 minutes. Serve warm with cream.

9th June

This is a very rich pudding with Russian origins. It goes beautifully with strawberries, which should be in season now, or raspberries if you have any in your freezer.

CHARLOTTE MALAKOFF
Serves 6 - 8

3 tbsp Grand Marnier + 1 tbsp water
20 - 24 sponge fingers
225g, 8oz butter
225g, 8oz caster sugar
225g, 8oz ground almonds
300ml, ½pt double cream, whipped

Mix 2 tablespoons of the Grand Marnier with the water and dip the smooth sides of the sponge fingers briefly in the liquid. Use them to line a 15cm, 6in charlotte mould. Cream together the butter and sugar and mix in the rest of the Grand Marnier and the almonds. Fold in the cream. Spoon into the lined mould. Trim the sponge fingers level with the filling. Chill for 2 or 3 hours before turning out.

10th June
MINT, LIME AND MELON SORBET
Serves 4 – 6

175g, 6oz caster sugar + 5 tbsp water
handful of fresh mint
1 ripe melon
grated rind and juice of 2 limes
2 egg whites (save yolks for tomorrow)

Put the sugar and water in a small saucepan and heat gently until the sugar dissolves. Bring to the boil and simmer for 5 minutes. Add the mint and allow to infuse for 30 minutes. Cut the melon up into chunks and purée. Strain the minty syrup onto the melon and add the lime rind and juice. Pour into a freezer container and freeze to the slushy stage. Take out and beat the mixture. Whisk the egg whites and fold them into the half frozen mixture. Freeze again until firm. Transfer to the fridge 30 minutes before serving.

11ᵗʰ June
STRAWBERRY LEMON CHEESECAKE
Serves 8

225g, 8oz digestive biscuits, crushed
75g, 3oz melted butter
225g, 8oz cream cheese
3 tbsp caster sugar
1 tsp vanilla essence
juice and grated rind of 1 lemon
2 eggs, separated + 2 egg yolks (from yesterday)
1 sachet gelatine and 2 tbsp warm water
200ml, 7fl oz double cream, whipped
225g, 8oz strawberries, halved

Mix the crushed biscuits with the butter and use to line a greased, loose-bottomed 23cm, 9in cake tin. Bake for 10 minutes at gas mark 2, 150°C (300°F) and allow to cool. To make the filling beat the cream cheese, sugar and vanilla essence until smooth. Add the lemon juice, rind and the egg yolks and beat again. Dissolve the gelatine in the water and stir into the mixture. Fold in the whipped cream. Beat the egg whites until stiff and fold them in too. Spoon over the biscuit base and chill. Just before serving, remove the cheesecake from the tin and cover the top with strawberries.

12ᵗʰ June

TOFFEE ICE CREAM
Serves 4 - 6

1 large tin of condensed milk
3 egg yolks (save whites for tomorrow & meringues the next day)
25g, 1oz caster sugar
250ml, 8fl oz whipping cream, whipped

Put the tin of condensed milk, unopened in a saucepan full of water and bring to the boil. Leave to simmer for two hours, topping up with water as it evaporates. Leave to cool before opening the tin.Whisk the egg yolks with the sugar until thick. Beat in the condensed milk and fold in the whipped cream. Freeze until firm – this ice cream remains lovely and soft with no further beating required.

13ᵗʰ June
BLACKCURRANT LEAF WATER ICE
Serves 6

200g, 7oz granulated sugar
juice and pared rind from 3 lemons
900ml, 1½pts water
4 handfuls of blackcurrant leaves
1 egg white

Dissolve the sugar in the lemon juice and the water. Bring to the boil and boil for 4 minutes. Add the blackcurrant leaves and lemon rind and leave to infuse for 40 minutes. Strain and press as much liquid as you can from the blackcurrant leaves. Pour into a freezer container and freeze until the slushy stage. Then beat the mixture, whisk the egg white and add to the half frozen mixture. Freeze until firm.

14ᵗʰ June
CARAMEL AND CRUSHED MERINGUE
WITH STRAWBERRIES
Serves 6 – 8

600ml, 1pt double cream
8 meringues, crushed
1 large tin of condensed milk, boiled in water for 2 hours
350g, 12oz strawberries, sliced

In a serving bowl spread a layer of cream, then a layer of meringue. Now spoon some of the cooked condensed milk over the meringues. If the condensed milk has become very thick you can stir in a spoonful of milk to thin it a little. Next add a layer of strawberries. Repeat the layers, finishing with cream. Chill well before serving.

15ᵗʰ June

ANGEL'S FOOD CAKE
Serves 4 – 6

4 egg whites (save yolks for tomorrow)
½ tsp cream of tartar
150g, 5oz caster sugar
40g, 1½oz plain flour
25g, 1oz cornflour
1 tsp vanilla essence
150ml, ¼pt crème fraîche
225g, 8oz strawberries, sliced

Whisk the egg whites until frothy, then add the cream of tartar and whisk until stiff. Sift the sugar and flours together and lightly fold into the egg white. Add the vanilla essence as well. Turn into a greased 20cm, 8in cake tin and bake in the oven at gas mark 3, 160°C (325°F) for 30 minutes. Turn out when cool. Top with crème fraîche and strawberries.

16ᵗʰ June

STRAWBERRY ICE CREAM
Serves 4

75g, 3oz granulated sugar
4 tbsp water
4 egg yolks (left over from yesterday)
150ml, ¼pt double cream, whipped
1 tbsp orange juice
350g, 12oz strawberries, puréed and sieved

Dissolve the sugar in the water. Bring to the boil and boil vigorously for a couple of minutes. Meanwhile whisk the egg yolks until pale and thick and gradually whisk in the sugar syrup. Whisk until cool and thick. Fold in the cream. Stir the orange juice into the strawberry purée and fold it into the egg yolk mixture. Pour into a freezer container and freeze until firm.

17ᵗʰ June

WHITE CHOCOLATE MOUSSE
Serves 6 – 8

275g, 10oz white chocolate
50g, 2oz unsalted butter
4 tbsp single cream
5 eggs, separated
1 tsp vanilla essence
150ml, ¼pt double cream, whipped

Melt the chocolate with the butter and cream in the microwave. Stir together until smooth. Beat in the egg yolks with the vanilla essence and leave to cool a little. Fold in the cream. Whisk the egg whites until firm and fold into the white chocolate mixture. Pour into a serving bowl and leave to set in the fridge. No gelatine is needed!

18ᵗʰ June

LEMON GERANIUM SORBET
Serves 4 - 6

75g, 3oz granulated sugar
4 lemon geranium leaves
juice of 1 lemon
1 egg white

Dissolve the sugar in 300ml, ½pt of water and boil for 2 or 3 minutes. Take off the heat and add the geranium leaves. Cover and leave to infuse for 30 minutes. Stir in the lemon juice and strain into a freezer container. When cold, freeze until slushy. Remove from the freezer and beat the mixture. Beat the egg white and fold it in. Return to the freezer and freeze until firm.

19th June

PEACHES WITH ELDERFLOWER-FLAVOURED STRAWBERRIES
Serves 6

225g, 8oz strawberries
2 tbsp elderflower cordial
175g, 6oz mascarpone
juice of ½ a lemon
6 ripe peaches, stoned and halved
2 tbsp golden caster sugar

Slice the strawberries and spoon the elderflower cordial over them. Allow them to marinade for 30 minutes, then gently fold them into the mascarpone. Brush the lemon juice over the halved peaches to prevent them discolouring. Transfer to a serving dish (one that can withstand a hot grill) and spoon the strawberry and mascarpone mixture into the holes left by the stones in the peaches. Sprinkle with the golden caster sugar. Place under a hot grill for a minute or until the mascarpone starts to melt. Serve immediately.

20th June

Save the left over egg whites for tomorrow's trifle.

NECTARINE CLAFOUTIS
Serves 4 – 6

50g, 2oz plain flour
50g, 2oz caster sugar
1 tbsp sunflower oil
2 eggs + 2 egg yolks
300ml, ½pt milk
450g, 1lb nectarines, halved and destoned
25g, 1oz butter, diced
1 tbsp demerara sugar

114

Stir the flour and caster sugar together. Beat in the oil, eggs, extra yolks and milk. Arrange the nectarines in a greased baking dish. Pour the batter over them and dot with the butter. Bake in the oven at gas mark 4, 180°C (350°F) for about 30 minutes until the batter is risen and browned. Sprinkle the tablespoon of demerara sugar over the batter and serve with cream.

21st June

It's the Summer Solstice, so why not celebrate with a pudding based on strawberries?

STRAWBERRY AND LEMON TIPSY TRIFLE
Serves 4 – 6

450g, 1lb strawberries, hulled and quartered
100g, 4oz macaroons, broken into pieces
90ml, 3fl oz sweet wine
3 tbsp set honey
1 tbsp brandy
2 tbsp lemon juice
150ml, ¼pt double cream
2 egg whites (from yesterday)

Mix the strawberries with the macaroons and put in a large glass bowl. Pour 2 tablespoons of the wine over them. Mix together the remaining wine, honey, brandy and lemon juice. Whip the cream and gradually whisk into the wine mixture. Whisk the egg whites and fold into the cream mixture. Pour over the strawberries. Cover and chill for an hour before serving.

22nd June

LEMON SYLLABUB
Serves 6

600ml, 1pt double cream
50g, 2oz caster sugar
grated rind and juice of 1 lemon
150ml, ¼pt dry sherry
150ml, ¼pt brandy

Beat all the ingredients together with a whisk for 15 minutes until very thick. Spoon into 6 glasses and chill until ready to serve.

23rd June

CHOCOLATE ICE CREAM WITH CHERRY SAUCE
Serves 6

100g, 4oz dark chocolate
1 small tin of condensed milk
½ tsp vanilla essence
300ml, ½pt double cream, lightly whipped

For the sauce
450g, 1lb cherries, halved and stoned
3 tbsp granulated sugar
150ml, ¼pt water
3 tbsp Kirsch

Dissolve the chocolate in the condensed milk in a bowl over a pan of simmering water. Remove from the heat and stir in the vanilla essence and 4 tablespoons of water. Leave to cool. Fold in the whipped cream, pour into a freezer container and freeze until firm. Put the cherries in a saucepan with the sugar and water. Simmer for about 5 minutes until the juices run, then turn up the heat and boil until the juice reduces and becomes syrupy. Remove from the heat and cool. Stir in the Kirsch. Serve with the ice cream.

24ᵗʰ June

This is a version of the French Savarin which is similar to a Rum Baba, but made without yeast.

FRUIT SAVARIN
Serves 4

3 eggs, separated
75g, 3oz caster sugar
4 tbsp milk
175g, 6oz self-raising flour
50g, 2oz butter, melted

Syrup
25g, 1oz granulated sugar
1 wine glass of rum or water and few drops of vanilla essence

Fruits of your choice such as sliced strawberries, bananas,
grapes, apples and oranges

First grease with butter a savarin mould or ring mould (1.2 litre or 2 pt capacity). Whisk the egg yolks with the caster sugar and milk. Sift the flour and fold into the egg yolk mixture. Fold in the melted butter. Lastly whisk the egg whites and fold them in. Spoon into the mould and bake in the oven at gas mark 4, 180°C (350°F) for 25 minutes. To make the syrup, dissolve the granulated sugar with the rum and vanilla essence over a low heat. Bring to the boil and boil for a couple of minutes. Turn out the savarin and prick with a skewer. Pour the boiling syrup evenly over the sponge and leave to soak in. Fill with fruits of your choice and serve.

25ᵗʰ June

STRAWBERRY MOUSSE
Serves 4 – 6

1 sachet gelatine + 2 tbsp water
3 eggs, separated
75g, 3oz caster sugar
225g, 8oz strawberries, puréed
150ml, ¼pt double cream, whipped

Dissolve the gelatine in the water over a very gentle heat. Whisk the egg yolks and sugar together until pale and thick. Whisk the egg whites until stiff. Fold the dissolved gelatine into the egg yolk mixture. Stir in the strawberry purée and cream. Lastly fold in the egg whites carefully and thoroughly. Spoon into a serving bowl and leave to set.

26ᵗʰ June

LEMON CARAMEL CREAM
Serves 4 - 6

Caramel
4 tbsp granulated sugar
2 tbsp water

50g, 2oz butter
225g, 8oz caster sugar
5 eggs, separated
50g, 2oz plain flour
grated rind and juice of 2 lemons

Make the caramel by dissolving the sugar in the water over a gentle heat. Boil until golden brown. Pour the caramel quickly into a soufflé dish. Cream the butter and sugar together. Beat the egg yolks into the mixture along with the flour. Add the rind and lemon juice. Whisk the egg whites and fold into the lemon mixture. Spoon over the caramel. Stand the dish in a roasting tin half filled with water and cook in the oven at gas mark 3, 160°C (325°F) for about 40 minutes.

27ᵗʰ June

Save the egg yolks for tomorrow's Melon Ice Cream.

ICED PEACH SOUFFLÉ
Serves 6 - 8

100g, 4oz granulated sugar
5 tbsp water
4 egg whites
450g, 1lb peaches, puréed and sieved
2 tsp lemon juice
300ml, ½pt double cream whipped

Dissolve the sugar in the water in a saucepan. Bring to the boil and boil for about 3 or 4 minutes. Meanwhile whisk the egg whites and gradually whisk in the hot sugar syrup. Continue to whisk until the meringue mixture is cool. Mix the lemon juice into the peach purée and fold into the meringue. Fold in the cream. Pour into a freezer container and freeze until firm.

28th June

MELON ICE CREAM
Serves 4

1 Ogen melon, halved and seeds removed
100g, 4oz caster sugar
4 egg yolks (from yesterday)
5 tbsp ginger wine
2 tbsp lemon juice
300ml, ½pt double cream, whipped

Scoop all the flesh from the melon into a saucepan and reserve the melon halves. Add the sugar and heat gently until the sugar has melted. Mash with a fork. Beat the egg yolks until thick and creamy and stir them into the melon. Continue cooking and whisking until the mixture is like thin cream. Leave to cool. Stir in the ginger wine and lemon juice and then fold in the whipped cream. Spoon into a freezer container and beat twice at hourly intervals to prevent ice crystals forming. Serve scoops of ice cream inside the melon shells if liked.

29th June

This is the Feast Day of St Peter and St Paul. St Peter was the Patron Saint of fishermen and the day is celebrated throughout the coastal regions of Chile. In Chile, as in Argentina, dulce de leche (sweet, soft toffee) is widely used in puddings. Here is a variation on a Chilean pastry filled with dulce de leche.

TOFFEE PASTRIES
Serves 6 – 8

3 tbsp demerara sugar
500g, 1lb puff pastry, rolled into 3 circles
1 jar dulce de leche or 1 tin condensed milk, boiled in water
for 2 hours
150ml, ¼pt double cream

Sprinkle the sugar over the puff pastry circles and press gently in. Bake the circles in the oven at gas mark 5, 190°C (375°F) for 10 minutes. Leave to cool for a few minutes. Mix the cream into two tablespoons of the dulce de leche. Use the rest of the dulce de leche to sandwich the two layers of pastry. Spread the combined cream and dulce de leche over the top.

30ᵗʰ June

PROFITEROLES WITH BUTTERSCOTCH SAUCE
Serves 6

Choux pastry
50g, 2oz butter
150ml, ¼pt water
60g, 2½oz plain flour, sifted
2 eggs, beaten

Filling
150ml, ¼pt whipping cream, whipped

Sauce
25g, 1oz butter
50g, 2oz dark brown sugar
150ml, ¼pt single cream

To make the profiteroles melt the butter in the water in a saucepan. Bring just to the boil and then add the flour all at once beating the flour until the mixture forms a ball. Cool slightly and then add the eggs a little at a time. Whisk the mixture until smooth and glossy. Put spoonfuls of this choux pastry on dampened baking sheets. Cook in a hot oven for 10 minutes and then lower the heat to gas mark 5, 190°C (375°F) and cook for a further 20 minutes until golden. Transfer to a rack to cool and slit each profiterole to let any air out. Fill with whipped cream. For the sauce, melt the butter and sugar and stir in the cream. Stir over a gentle heat until the sauce bubbles and becomes glossy. Pour over the profiteroles and serve.

1ˢᵗ July

This is Canada Day. Here is a Canadian inspired pudding.

SOURED CREAM RAISIN AND PECAN PIE
Serves 6 – 8

Double quantity sweet shortcrust pastry (see page 5)
225g, 8oz raisins
150ml, ¼pt soured cream
1 tsp ground cinnamon
¼ tsp ground cloves + ¼ tsp freshly grated nutmeg
2 eggs
50g, 2oz dark brown sugar
50g, 2oz pecans, chopped

Roll out the pastry into two circles. Use one half to line a greased 23cm, 9in flan tin. To make the filling put the raisins in a bowl and stir in the soured cream and spices. Beat the eggs and stir into the cream and raisin mixture. Stir in the brown sugar and pecans. Pour into the pastry case. Use the other circle of pastry as a lid and press down to join the 2 circles together. Prick with a fork and brush with a little milk. Bake in the oven at gas mark 4, 180°C (350°F) for 30 minutes. Serve warm or cold.

2ⁿᵈ July

Blackcurrants should just be ripening up now.

BLACKCURRANT AND RICOTTA DESSERT
Serves 4

225g, 8oz blackcurrants
50g, 2oz caster sugar
1 tsp cornflour
100g, 4oz ricotta cheese
150ml, ¼pt Greek yoghurt
2 tbsp honey

Cook the blackcurrants in a saucepan with the sugar and a tablespoon of water for about 10 minutes. Mix the cornflour to a paste with a few drops of water and blend into the blackcurrant mixture. Cook for a couple more minutes. Beat together the ricotta cheese, Greek yoghurt and honey and place in a serving bowl. Pour the blackcurrant mixture over the top and swirl it around with a knife to give a marbled effect. Serve at once.

3rd July

RED BERRY JELLY
Serves 8

1½ sachets of gelatine
225g, 8oz caster sugar
300ml, ½pt water
350g, 12oz raspberries
350g, 12oz strawberries, sliced
350g, 12oz redcurrants
3 tbsp Cassis

Sprinkle the gelatine over 4 tablespoons of the water. Meanwhile mix the sugar and the rest of the water in a saucepan and bring to the boil, stirring until the sugar dissolves. Simmer for 5 minutes then add all the fruit and bring back to the boil. Remove from the heat and add the Cassis. Warm the gelatine until it dissolves and stir into the hot fruit. Divide the mixture between ramekin dishes or spoon into a serving bowl. Leave to set.

4ᵗʰ *July*

This is an American inspired pudding to celebrate American Independence Day. This pudding comes from the Ozark mountains in Missouri and was apparently a great favourite of President and Mrs Truman (Harry Truman was President of the US between 1945 and 1953).

OZARK PUDDING
Serves 4 – 6

1 egg
175g, 6oz caster sugar
few drops vanilla essence
40g, 1½oz plain flour, sifted
1 tsp baking powder
1 large cooking apple, peeled, cored and chopped
50g, 2oz walnuts, chopped

Beat together the egg, sugar and vanilla essence. Sift the flour and baking powder and fold into the egg mixture. Fold in the apple and walnuts and pour into a greased 1.2 litre, 2pt baking dish. Bake in the oven at gas mark 3, 160°C (325°F) for 30 minutes. Serve with cream or Greek yoghurt.

5ᵗʰ *July*

Blackcurrants and pears go rather well together and, contrary to what you might expect, the blackcurrants don't swamp the pears.

PEAR AND BLACKCURRANT STREUSEL PIE
Serves 6 - 8

Shortcrust pastry (see page 5)
450g, 1lb pears, peeled, cored and sliced
225g, 8oz blackcurrants
75g, 3oz plain flour

25g, 1oz ground almonds
100g, 4oz caster sugar
50g, 2oz butter
150ml, ¼pt double cream
50g, 2oz caster sugar for sprinkling
pinch of nutmeg

Roll out the pastry and use to line a greased 20cm, 8in round deep pie dish. Make the filling by mixing the sliced pears and blackcurrants together. Stir together the flour, almonds and sugar and rub in the butter using your fingertips. Sprinkle half this mixture over the pastry. Spread the pears and blackcurrants evenly over this. Pour over the cream. Spoon over the remaining rubbed-in mixture and sprinkle with the caster sugar and nutmeg. Bake in a preheated oven at gas mark 6, 200°C (400°F) for 40 minutes. Allow to cool slightly before serving.

6*th* *July*

RASPBERRY AND WATERMELON CREAM ICE
Serves 4 – 6

4 tbsp clear honey
juice of ½ a lemon
150ml, ¼pt whipping cream
150ml, ¼pt Greek yoghurt
225g, 8oz raspberries
1 watermelon
caster sugar to taste

Whisk the honey and lemon juice together. Whip the cream. Fold the honey and lemon into the cream and yoghurt. Fold in the raspberries. Cut the watermelon in half. Scoop out the flesh, remove the seeds and purée the flesh. Add this to the cream mixture. Have a taste and add some caster sugar if it is still not sweet enough. Pour into a freezer container and freeze beating twice at hourly intervals.

7ᵗʰ July

Around this date in 1746 Flora MacDonald is reputed to have been halfway through a dish of Scottish Flummery when she was arrested. She had been helping Bonnie Prince Charlie to escape – he had been on the run ever since his defeat at the Battle of Culloden in April. On 27ᵗʰ June Flora had set sail for Skye with a manservant (Charles's companion Captain O'Neill), an Irish spinning maid, Betty Burke (Charles in disguise), and a boat's crew of six men. They landed at what is now called Prince Charles's Point, a couple of miles north of Uig. From there they went overland to Portree, so that Charles could travel to Raasay in the hope of being picked up by a French warship. Charles did eventually escape to France. Flora unfortunately was arrested after one of the boatmen talked about the strange maid who had travelled with them. She was imprisoned, first in Dunstaffnage Castle, then in the Tower of London.

SCOTTISH FLUMMERY
Serves 4

1 tbsp medium oatmeal
300ml, ½pt double cream
3 tbsp clear honey
4 tbsp whisky
juice of ½ a lemon

Heat the oatmeal in a heavy based saucepan until it turns brown. Beat the cream and fold in the honey. Stir in the whisky and the lemon juice. Divide the mixture between four glasses and sprinkle with the oatmeal.

8ᵗʰ July

BLACKCURRANT SPONGE PUDDING
Serves 4 - 6

225g, 8oz blackcurrants
50g, 2oz granulated sugar

For the sponge
100g, 4oz self-raising flour
1 tsp baking powder
2 eggs
100g, 4oz caster sugar
100g, 4oz butter

Spread the blackcurrants and sugar over the base of a greased round 20cm, 8in ovenproof dish. Put the flour, baking powder, eggs, sugar and butter in a food processor and process until you have a smooth mixture. Spread over the top of the blackcurrants and cook in a preheated oven at gas mark 4, 180°C (350°F) for 35 to 40 minutes. Serve hot with cream or ice cream.

9ᵗʰ July

This recipe uses 2 egg yolks. Save the egg whites for tomorrow's pavlova.

MASCARPONE ICE CREAM WITH
BLACKCURRANT AND CHESTNUT SAUCE
Serves 6

2 egg yolks
50g, 2oz icing sugar
225g, 8oz mascarpone
2 tsp vanilla essence

For the sauce
225g, 8oz blackcurrants, puréed and sieved
100g, 4oz sweetened chestnut purée (or unsweetened – add 50g,
2oz brown sugar)

Whisk together the egg yolks and icing sugar until really thick. Beat the mascarpone and vanilla essence into the egg yolk mixture. Transfer to a freezer container and freeze until firm. Mix the chestnut purée and blackcurrant juice together and serve with the ice cream.

10ᵗʰ July

Save extra egg yolks for tomorrow's ice cream.

PEAR AND RASPBERRY PAVLOVA
Serves 6 – 8

4 egg whites (2 saved from yesterday)
225g, 8oz caster sugar
1 tsp cornflour, sifted
1 tsp white wine vinegar
1 tsp vanilla essence

For the topping
150ml, ¼pt whipping cream + 150ml, ¼pt soured cream
225g, 8oz raspberries
50g, 2oz granulated sugar
225g, 8oz pears, peeled, cored and sliced

To make the pavlova, beat the egg whites until stiff. Gradually beat in the sugar, a little at a time. Sprinkle the cornflour, vinegar and vanilla over the mixture and fold in carefully. Make a circle with the meringue mixture on a large greased baking sheet. Bake for an hour at gas mark 1, 140°C (275°F). The pavlova should be crisp on the outside with a soft marshmallow centre. Whip the cream with the soured cream. Spread this over the meringue. Cook the raspberries with the sugar over a gentle heat until the juices run. Add the pears and cook for a couple more minutes. Carefully pour the pear slices and raspberries over the cream and serve at once.

11ᵗʰ July

If you use yesterday's egg yolks, you will need one more and can save the egg white for tomorrow's sorbet.

RASPBERRY ICE CREAM
Serves 6 – 8

450g, 1lb raspberries, puréed and sieved
2 tbsp icing sugar + a squeeze of lemon juice

75g, 3oz granulated sugar + 120ml, 4fl oz water
3 egg yolks
300ml, ½pt double cream

Add the icing sugar and lemon juice to the sieved raspberries. Dissolve the sugar in the water and then bring to the boil and keep it boiling for a couple of minutes. Meanwhile whisk the egg yolks until pale and thick and then slowly whisk in the sugar syrup in a steady stream. Continue to whisk the mixture as it cools. Fold the egg yolk mixture into the raspberry purée. Whip the cream and fold that in too. Stir until the mixture is smooth. Pour into a freezer container and freeze until firm.

12ᵗʰ July

On this day events are held across Northern Ireland to commemorate victory at the Battle of the Boyne. It was here that Protestant William of Orange beat Catholic James II in 1690. The Orange Order is the largest Protestant organisation in Northern Ireland. Here is an Irish pudding to celebrate.

COFFEE SORBET WITH WHITE CHOCOLATE SAUCE
Serves 4

100g, 4oz caster sugar + 50g, 2oz dark brown sugar
2 tbsp instant coffee + 300ml, ½pt water
1 tbsp Baileys Irish cream
1 egg white (from yesterday)

Sauce
50g, 2oz white chocolate + 5 tbsp single cream

Put the sugars, coffee and water in a saucepan and stir over a gentle heat until the sugars have dissolved. Bring to the boil and simmer for 3 minutes. Allow to cool, stir in the Baileys, pour into a freezer container and freeze until slushy. Remove from the freezer, whisk the mixture thoroughly and in a separate bowl whisk the egg white. Fold it into the coffee mixture and return to the freezer. To make the sauce melt the chocolate and cream together over a low heat and stir until smooth. Serve the sorbet with the sauce.

13ᵗʰ *July*

RASPBERRY AND CHOCOLATE CREAM PUDDING
Serves 4 – 6

1 whisked sponge (see page 6)
2 tbsp golden syrup mixed with 100ml, 3fl oz boiling water
225g, 8oz raspberries
100g, 4oz plain chocolate
200ml, 7fl oz double cream

Fit the sponge into the bottom of a glass bowl about 20cm, 8in in diameter. Pour the golden syrup mixture over the sponge. Spread the raspberries over the top. Heat the cream and add the chocolate. Stir until it melts into the cream. Leave to cool and spread over the raspberries.

14ᵗʰ *July*

This is Bastille Day and is a National Day in France. It commemorates the storming of Bastille Prison in 1789 which was the beginning of The French Revolution. So why not celebrate with a French pudding?

SAINT EMILION AU CHOCOLAT
Serves 6 - 8

450g, 1lb macaroons
4 tbsp rum
100g, 4oz butter
100g, 4oz caster sugar
300ml, ½pt milk
1 egg yolk
225g, 8oz plain chocolate
1 tbsp water

Soak the macaroons in the rum. Cream together the butter and sugar. Warm the milk and beat in the egg yolk. Melt the chocolate, stir in the water and then the milk and egg mixture. Beat in the creamed butter and sugar. Stir everything together until well blended. Place a layer of the chocolate mixture in a serving dish. Cover with a layer of macaroons and continue the layers finishing with macaroons. Chill before serving.

15ᵗʰ *July*

It's St Swithin's Day. A good crop of apples is forecast if rain falls in the orchard today. Celebrate with an apple-based pudding.

GOLDEN APPLE PUDDING
Serves 4 – 6

450g, 1lb cooking apples, peeled and cored
grated rind and juice of 1 lemon
50g, 2oz brown breadcrumbs
25g, 1oz butter, melted
150g, 5oz caster sugar
2 eggs, separated

Grate the apples into a bowl. Stir in the grated lemon rind and juice, breadcrumbs, melted butter, 75g, 3oz of the caster sugar and the egg yolks. Mix well together. Whisk the egg whites until stiff. Whisk in the remaining 50g, 2oz of sugar and then fold this meringue mixture into the apple mixture. Turn into a round 20cm, 8in ovenproof dish and bake in the oven at gas mark 4, 180°C (350°F) for 45 minutes. Serve warm.

16ᵗʰ July

It's the height of summer so celebrate with a Summer Pudding.

TRADITIONAL SUMMER PUDDING
Serves 6

900g, 2lb summer fruits such as black and redcurrants,
raspberries, strawberries
175g, 6oz caster sugar
8 – 10 slices wholemeal bread, crusts removed

Cook the black and redcurrants adding 2 tablespoons of water and the sugar. After a few minutes add the raspberries and cook for a couple more minutes. Lastly add the strawberries and turn off the heat. Use the slices of bread to line a 1.2 litre, 2 pint basin including the bottom. Pour the cooked fruit into the bowl with all the juices. Press a slice of bread down on top and put a plate on top with a weight. Refrigerate overnight and when ready to serve, run a knife around the sides and turn the pudding out. Serve with cream or crème fraîche.

17ᵗʰ July

BLACKCURRANT CLAFOUTIS
Serves 6

100g, 4oz plain flour
2 eggs
300ml, ½pt milk
25g, 1oz butter
450g, 1lb blackcurrants
75g, 3oz caster sugar

Sift the flour into a bowl and make a well in the centre. Crack one whole egg and one egg yolk into the well and add half the milk. Stir the liquid in with a wooden spoon, gradually drawing in the flour.

Beat to a smooth batter and stir in the remaining milk. Whisk the egg white and fold it in. Butter a baking dish and put it in the oven at gas mark 6, 200°C (400°F) to warm up. Remove and scatter the blackcurrants over the base. Immediately pour over the batter and return to the oven for 30 minutes or until risen and golden brown. Sprinkle the caster sugar all over the top of the batter and serve with cream.

18ᵗʰ July

BAKED PEACHES WITH RASPBERRIES
Serves 8

8 peaches
8 macaroons, crushed
2 egg yolks
2 tbsp Marsala
50g, 2oz chopped almonds
100g, 4oz caster sugar
grated rind of ½ a lemon
225g, 8oz raspberries
sprinkling of white wine
knob of butter

Cut the peaches in half and remove the stones. Hollow out some of the flesh and reserve. Grease an ovenproof dish and place the peach halves on it. Mix the peach flesh with the crushed macaroons and add the egg yolks, Marsala, almonds, sugar and grated lemon rind. Mix well and stuff a little mixture into each peach half. Scatter the raspberries over and around the peaches. Dot with butter and sprinkle with white wine. Cook in the oven at gas mark 5, 190°C (375°F) for about 20 minutes. Serve hot.

Make meringue biscuits with the 2 left over egg whites (see page 204).

19ᵗʰ July

The flavour of mint goes rather well with blackcurrants and, if you grow your own blackcurrants and mint, both should be abundant at this time of year.

MINT AND BLACKCURRANT MOUSSE
Serves 4 – 6

450g, 1lb blackcurrants
175g, 6oz caster sugar
2 handfuls of fresh mint
3 eggs, separated
juice of 1 lemon
1 sachet gelatine
300ml, ½pt double cream, whipped

Put the blackcurrants in a saucepan and cook with 50g, 2oz of the sugar over a gentle heat until the juices begin to run and they are soft. Then purée the blackcurrants with the mint leaves and sieve to remove the pips. Dissolve the gelatine in the lemon juice over a gentle heat. Whisk the egg yolks with the remaining sugar until thick and creamy and whisk the gelatine mixture into the yolks. Fold in the blackcurrant purée. Leave until beginning to set and then gently fold in the cream. Lastly whisk the egg whites until stiff and fold them in. Pour into a serving bowl and allow to set in the fridge.

20ᵗʰ July

This is St Margaret's Day. Her pet name was St Peg and it was traditional to eat a plum pudding to celebrate her Feast Day – this was called Heg Peg Dump and was traditionally celebrated in Gloucestershire.

HEG PEG DUMP
Serves 4 – 6

225g, 8oz self-raising flour
100g, 4oz shredded suet
1 tsp baking powder
150ml, ¼pt water

Filling
450g, 1lb plums, halved and stoned
225g, 8oz cooking apples, cored, peeled and sliced
175g, 6oz granulated sugar
1 tbsp breadcrumbs
1 tbsp water

Mix the flour, suet and baking powder with enough water to make a soft dough. Knead until smooth. Roll out the dough and line a greased 1.2 litre, 2 pint pudding basin with it. Fill with layers of plums and apples, mixed with the sugar, breadcrumbs and water. Make a lid with the remaining pastry. Cover with greaseproof paper and steam in the normal way for 3 hours.

21ˢᵗ July

BLUEBERRY ICE CREAM
Serves 4

2 eggs, separated
75g, 3oz caster sugar
3 tbsp blackcurrant juice such as Ribena
300ml, ½pt double cream, whipped
225g, 8oz blueberries

Whisk the egg yolks and sugar until pale and thick and then add the blackcurrant juice and whisk again. Fold the cream into the egg yolk mixture and then the blueberries. Whisk the egg whites and fold them in too. Spoon into a freezer container and freeze. Remove from the freezer about 20 minutes before serving.

22nd July

BLACKCURRANT AND CHOCOLATE TRIFLE
Serves 6 – 8

For the sponge
100g, 4oz butter
100g, 4oz caster sugar
100g, 4oz self-raising flour
2 eggs

350g, 12oz blackcurrants
100g, 4oz granulated sugar
½ tsp ground cinnamon
100g, 4oz plain chocolate
15g, ½oz butter
2 eggs, separated
300ml, ½pt double cream, whipped

To make the sponge, cream together the butter and sugar. Gradually add the eggs and flour. Beat together well and spoon into a greased 20cm, 8in cake tin. Bake in the oven at gas mark 4, 180°C (350°F) for about 25 minutes. Turn out, break into pieces and use to cover the base of a 20cm, 8in round pyrex dish. Cook the blackcurrants with the sugar, a couple of tablespoons of water and the cinnamon until softened. Pour over the sponge. Melt the chocolate with the butter over a gentle heat. Beat the egg yolks into the chocolate mixture. Whisk the egg whites and fold them in as well. Spread over the blackcurrants. Cover with the cream. Chill until ready to serve.

23rd *July*

Save the egg yolks for tomorrow's ice cream.

BLUEBERRY AND VANILLA PAVLOVA
Serves 6 – 8

4 egg whites
225g, 8oz caster sugar
1 tsp vanilla essence
1 tsp cornflour
1 tsp white wine vinegar
pinch of cream of tartar

Topping
225g, 8oz blueberries
25g, 1oz caster sugar
225g, 8oz mascarpone
2 tbsp light muscovado sugar
150ml, ¼pt Greek yoghurt
1 tbsp lemon juice

To make the pavlova whisk the egg whites and continue whisking them while gradually adding the caster sugar. Fold in the vanilla essence, vinegar, cornflour and cream of tartar. Spread the mixture in a circle on a greased baking sheet and bake in a preheated oven at gas mark 4, 180°C (350°F) for 5 minutes then reduce to gas mark 1, 140°C (275°F) and cook for an hour. Transfer to a serving plate. Put the blueberries in a small saucepan with the sugar. Heat gently until the sugar dissolves and the blueberries soften. Leave to cool. Beat the mascarpone and stir in the sugar, yoghurt and lemon juice. Spread the mascarpone mixture over the pavlova and cover with the blueberries.

24th July

ZABAGLIONE ICE CREAM
WITH RASPBERRY AND BLACKCURRANT SAUCE
Serves 6 – 8

4 egg yolks (from yesterday)
75g, 3oz caster sugar
120ml, 4fl oz Marsala
300ml, ½pt double cream

For the sauce
100g, 4oz blackcurrants
75g, 3oz granulated sugar
100g, 4oz raspberries
1 tbsp Cassis

Put the egg yolks and sugar in a bowl and beat over a saucepan of simmering water until very pale and thick. Then gradually add the Marsala, a tablespoon at a time, while you continue to whisk. You will need to whisk for about 20 minutes. You must add the Marsala slowly and allow the mixture to thicken or it will separate. Whip the double cream until fairly thick and gently fold into the egg mixture. Pour into a freezer container and freeze until firm. For the sauce gently heat the blackcurrants with the sugar until the juices begin to run. Add the raspberries and cook for a couple more minutes. Then purée and sieve the fruit. Stir in the Cassis. Serve warm or cold with the ice cream.

25th July

This is St James's day, St James being the Patron Saint of Spain. The shrine of St James is at Santiago de Compostela and this tart was dedicated to St James. A true tart should bear the cross of the knights of St James.

GALICIAN ALMOND TART – TARTA DE SANTIAGO
Serves 6

Sweet shortcrust pastry (see page 5)
4 eggs
225g, 8oz caster sugar
grated rind of 1 lemon
225g, 8oz ground almonds
pinch of ground cinnamon

Roll out the pastry and use to line a greased 20cm, 8in flan dish. Beat the eggs and sugar together until thick. Fold in the grated lemon rind, ground almonds and cinnamon. Pour over the pastry case and bake in the oven at gas mark 4, 180°C (350°F) for about 30 minutes. Leave to cool and dust with icing sugar before serving.

26ᵗʰ July

ICED REDCURRANT MERINGUE
Serves 6 – 8

350g, 12oz redcurrants
50g, 2oz icing sugar
3 tbsp lemon juice
300ml, ½pt double cream
150ml, ¼pt single cream
8 meringues
225g, 8oz raspberries

Mix the redcurrants with the icing sugar and lemon juice. Purée and sieve them. Whip the creams together. Break up the meringues and mix with the cream. Stir the redcurrant purée into the meringue mixture to give a marbled effect. Pour into a 900ml, 1½pt ring mould and freeze for about 6 hours. Remove from the freezer and turn out. Pile the raspberries in the centre of the ring and serve.

27ᵗʰ July

BLUEBERRY CHEESECAKE
Serves 6 - 8

Sweet shortcrust pastry (see page 5)
100g, 4oz butter
100g, 4oz caster sugar
3 eggs, beaten
1 tbsp plain flour
grated rind and juice of 2 small lemons
1 tsp vanilla essence
450g, 1lb cream cheese
2 tbsp milk

Topping
150ml, ¼pt double cream
350g, 12oz blueberries

Roll out the pastry and line the bottom and sides of a greased 20cm, 8in springform cake tin. Chill while you make the filling. Cream the butter and sugar together and gradually add the eggs and the flour. Beat in the lemon rind, juice and vanilla essence. In another bowl beat the cream cheese and milk and then add to the butter mixture and beat well together. Pour this into the chilled pastry case and bake at gas mark 3, 160°C (325°F) for about an hour or until set and golden on top. Turn the oven off and allow to cool gradually in the oven – this will help stop any cracks appearing. Turn out of the tin, whip the cream and spread over the cheesecake. Arrange the blueberries over the cream and serve.

28th July

This is a Danish pudding – a light purée of summer fruits, slightly thickened.

RODGROD MED FLODE
Serves 4 - 6

225g, 8oz redcurrants
100g, 4oz raspberries
50g, 2oz blackcurrants
100g, 4oz caster sugar
25g, 1oz cornflour
6 tbsp Greek yoghurt

Put the fruit in a saucepan with the sugar and enough water just to cover. Simmer over a low heat until the fruit is soft, then purée and sieve the fruit. Blend a little of the cornflour with some of the fruit juice stirring to make a smooth paste. Add to the pan and stir over a low heat until it thickens. Allow to cool, stirring every so often to stop a skin forming. Serve with dollops of Greek yoghurt or swirl the yoghurt through the purée.

29th July

This is the feast day of St Martha. She is the Patron Saint of housewives, cooks and innkeepers, so here is a special pudding to help you celebrate all the cooks in your household. The addition of blackcurrants underneath the sponge topping makes a nice surprise.

LEMON AND BLACKCURRANT SURPRISE PUDDING
Serves 6 - 8

450g, 1lb blackcurrants
50g, 2oz brown sugar
75g, 3oz butter
225g, 8oz caster sugar
grated rind of 2 lemons
6 eggs, separated
50g, 2oz plain flour
300ml, ½pt milk

Put the blackcurrants in the bottom of a recangular or oval ovenproof dish (a tin works the best although not so elegant as a china dish) and sprinkle with the brown sugar. Cream the butter and caster sugar together. Beat in the grated lemon rind and then the egg yolks one at a time. Stir in the flour and milk. Whisk the egg whites until stiff and fold them in making sure all is well incorporated. Pour on top of the blackcurrants. Stand the dish in a roasting tin half filled with water. Bake in the oven at gas mark 4, 180°C (350°F) for about 40 minutes or until the sponge topping is cooked. Serve warm with cream.

30ᵗʰ July

BLUEBERRY PIE
Serves 4 - 6

75g, 3oz caster sugar
3 tbsp cornflour
grated rind and juice of ½ an orange
grated rind of ½ a lemon
450g, 1lb blueberries
½ tsp ground cinnamon
shortcrust pastry (see page 5)
beaten egg to glaze
sprinkling of caster sugar

Mix the sugar, cornflour, orange juice and orange and lemon rinds into the blueberries and sprinkle on the cinnamon. Transfer to a 20cm, 8in pie dish. Roll out the pastry to form a lid and cover the blueberries. Glaze with the beaten egg and sprinkle with caster sugar. Bake in the oven at gas mark 4, 180°C (350°F) for 30 minutes and serve hot with cream.

31st July

This is a really easy ice cream to make. Serve with Blackcurrant Kissel or a butterscotch sauce (see page 121).

VANILLA ICE CREAM WITH BLACKCURRANT KISSEL
Serves 6 - 8

4 eggs, separated
100g, 4oz icing sugar
1 tsp vanilla essence
300ml, ½pt double cream

For the Kissel
450g, 1lb blackcurrants
3 tbsp clear honey
juice of 1 lemon
pinch of ground nutmeg
1 – 2 tbsp caster sugar
25g, 1oz wholemeal plain flour

Whisk the egg yolks with half the icing sugar until thick and pale. Whisk the egg whites until stiff then gradually whisk in the remaining icing sugar, a small amount at a time. Whisk the double cream with the vanilla essence until thick. Stir the cream into the egg yolk mixture and then fold in the egg whites. Make sure everything is thoroughly blended and then transfer to a freezer container. Freeze until firm.

For the Kissel put the blackcurrants, honey and lemon juice into a saucepan with enough cold water just to cover the fruit. Heat gently and simmer until the fruit is soft. Sieve the fruit and add a pinch of nutmeg. At this stage taste the purée. If it is too tart add the caster sugar. Put the flour into a bowl and stir in some of the blackcurrant mixture to make a paste. Mix this paste into the rest of the purée and stir over a low heat until thickened. Serve with the ice cream.

1ˢᵗ August

This is Lammas Day which traditionally marked the end of the growing season. Lammas means loaf-mass – loaves of bread were baked with grain from the first harvest and laid on the church altar as offerings. Here is a Bread and Butter Pudding to celebrate.

BREAD AND BUTTER PUDDING
Serves 4

3 eggs
300ml, ½pt single cream
100g, 4oz light brown sugar
2 tbsp raisins + 2 tbsp currants
grated rind of 1 lemon and 1 orange
6 slices of bread, buttered and cut into squares

Mix the eggs with the cream and sugar. Pour into a shallow ovenproof dish. Mix together the raisins, currants and grated rind. Spoon into the dish and scatter on the squares of buttered bread. Leave to soak in for an hour and then cook in the oven at gas mark 4, 180°C (350°F) for 40 minutes.

2ⁿᵈ August

RASPBERRY AND REDCURRANT MOUSSE
Serves 4 – 6

225g, 8oz raspberries
225g, 8oz redcurrants
175g, 6oz caster sugar
2 egg whites (save egg yolks for tomorrow)

Sieve the raspberries and redcurrants to remove all pips. Stir in the sugar. Whisk the egg whites until stiff and fold into the purée. In a saucepan over a low heat whisk the mixture for about 3 minutes until the mixture thickens and starts to rise. Pour into glasses or a serving bowl and leave to cool before serving. If left for a while some of the juice will separate and sink to the bottom but can be whipped up again before serving.

3rd August

In the sixteenth century Marquis Muzio Frangipani created a perfume from almonds that was used for scenting gloves and became popular in Paris. Parisian pastry cooks, inspired by the scent, flavoured a topping for tarts with almonds and called it 'frangipane'.

BLUEBERRY FRANGIPANE TART
Serves 8

For the base
175g, 6oz plain flour
100g, 4oz caster sugar
100g, 4oz butter

For the filling
200g, 7oz butter
200g, 7oz caster sugar
1 egg and 2 egg yolks (from yesterday)
6 tbsp plain flour, sieved
175g, 6oz ground almonds
4 tbsp double cream
225g, 8oz blueberries

To make the base, place the flour and sugar in a bowl and rub in the butter. Add a tablespoon of water and knead together until you have a soft dough. Chill for 30 minutes. Roll out the dough and line a greased 23cm, 9in flan tin. Prick and bake in the oven at gas mark 5, 190°C (375°F) for 15 minutes. To make the filling, cream together the butter and sugar. Beat in the egg and egg yolks and stir in the flour, almonds and cream. Spread the blueberries over the base of the pastry and spoon the filling on top. Bake in the oven at gas mark 4, 180°C (350°F) for about 45 minutes or until the topping has set.

4ᵗʰ August

BLACKCURRANT AND LIME SORBET
Serves 4 – 6

300ml, ½pt water + 175g, 6oz granulated sugar
juice of 1 lime
450g, 1lb blackcurrants
2 egg whites (save 1 yolk for tomorrow)

Put the water and sugar in a saucepan and heat gently until the sugar has dissolved. Bring to the boil and boil for 5 minutes until syrupy. Remove from the heat, stir in the lime juice and leave to cool. Meanwhile put the blackcurrants in a saucepan and heat gently until the juices start to run, which should be after about 5 minutes. Sieve the blackcurrants and stir the blackcurrant purée into the cooled syrup. Freeze for an hour and then remove the slushy blackcurrant mixture and beat thoroughly. Whisk the egg whites until stiff and fold these into the blackcurrant mixture. Freeze until firm.

5ᵗʰ August

MULBERRY CLAFOUTIS
Serves 4 – 6

50g, 2oz plain flour
50g, 2oz + 1 tbsp caster sugar
1 tbsp sunflower oil
2 eggs + 1 egg yolk (from yesterday)
300ml, ½pt milk
450g, 1lb mulberries
25g, 1oz butter, diced

Stir the flour and caster sugar together. Beat in the oil, eggs and milk. Arrange the mulberries in a greased baking dish. Pour the batter over them and dot with the butter. Bake in the oven at gas mark 4, 180°C (350°F) for about 30 minutes until the batter is risen and browned. Sprinkle the tablespoon of caster sugar over the batter and serve with cream.

6ᵗʰ August

The first Sunday in August is the traditional date of Cherry Pie Sunday, when the last of the black cherries would be gathered. This tart comes from the village of Ripe in the Sussex South Downs. Ripe was where a pie feast used to be held to celebrate the cherry harvest.

RIPE TART
Serves 6 - 8

For the pastry
225g, 8oz plain flour + 25g, 1oz cornflour
1 tsp icing sugar
100g, 4oz butter
1 egg yolk (save the white for tomorrow)

450g, 1lb cherries
100g, 4oz icing sugar
2 eggs
75g, 3oz ground almonds
few drops of almond essence

Make the pastry by combining all the ingredients in a processor, adding a little cold water. Bind together, form into a ball, roll out and use to line a 23cm, 9in flan tin. Prick and bake blind in the oven at gas mark 4, 180°C (350°F) for 10 minutes. Arrange the cherries over the base. Mix together the icing sugar, eggs, ground almonds and almond essence. Pour over the cherries. Return to the oven for 30 minutes until the top is golden.

7ᵗʰ August

MELON AND PEACH SORBET
Serves 6 – 8

1 small cantaloupe melon
3 peaches, skinned and cut into slices
100g, 4oz granulated sugar
6 tbsp water

2 tbsp peach liqueur, optional
2 egg whites (save the extra yolk for tomorrow)

Chop the melon into chunks and purée with the peach slices. Put the sugar and water in a small saucepan over a gentle heat and stir until the sugar has dissolved. Bring the syrup to the boil, simmer for 3 minutes and then leave to cool. Stir together the purée, sugar syrup and liqueur. Transfer to a freezer container. Freeze until the slushy stage and then beat to break down ice crystals. Whisk the egg white until stiff and fold into the sorbet. Freeze again until firm.

8ᵗʰ August

Tayberries are in season now. They were first cultivated in Scotland where raspberries were crossed with blackberries.

TAYBERRY AND CHOCOLATE TARTLETS
Makes 4 – 5 tartlets

For the pastry
225g, 8oz plain flour
150g, 5oz butter
3 tbsp icing sugar
1 egg yolk (saved from yesterday)

350g, 12oz tayberries
225g, 8oz fromage frais
175g, 6oz Greek yoghurt
100g, 4oz milk chocolate
icing sugar for dusting

Put all the ingredients for the pastry into a food processor and process until the mixture binds together. Chill for 30 minutes. Then roll out into rounds and fit into the base of 4 or 5 greased tartlet tins. Prick and bake blind in the oven at gas mark 4, 180°C (350°F) for 10 minutes and then cool. Divide the tayberries between the tartlets. To make the topping mix together the fromage frais and yoghurt. Melt the chocolate and quickly stir into the fromage frais mixture. It will start setting immediately. Spoon over the tayberries. Dust with icing sugar and serve.

9th August

RICE PUDDING WITH RASPBERRY SAUCE
Serves 4 – 6

900ml, 1½pts milk
175g, 6oz pudding rice
1 tsp vanilla essence
2 tbsp caster sugar
100ml, 3fl oz double cream

For the sauce
175g, 6oz raspberries
2 tbsp icing sugar
2 tsp cornflour, stirred to a paste with a little water

This rice pudding is cooked on the hob. Bring the milk to the boil in a large saucepan and stir in the rice and vanilla essence. Cover the pan, lower the heat and simmer for 30 minutes, making sure the rice doesn't stick. After 30 minutes stir in the sugar and cream. You can now pour the rice pudding into a ring mould and leave to set or serve as it is. To make the raspberry sauce, cook the raspberries with the icing sugar for a few minutes. Sieve to remove pips, return to the saucepan and stir in the cornflour. Cook to thicken the sauce. Serve the hot sauce with the cold rice pudding.

10th August

BLUEBERRY AND NECTARINE COBBLER
Serves 6

6 nectarines, stoned and sliced
225g, 8oz blueberries
50g, 2oz light muscovado sugar
225g, 8oz mascarpone

For the cobbler
225g, 8oz self-raising flour
75g, 3oz butter
50g, 2oz light muscovado sugar
grated rind of 1 lemon
150ml, ¼pt crème fraîche

Put the nectarine slices in an ovenproof dish and add the blueberries. Sprinkle over the sugar and spoon over the mascarpone. To make the cobbler rub the butter into the flour, stir in the sugar and grated lemon. Make a well in the centre and add the yoghurt. Mix the yoghurt in gradually until everything is well combined. Spoon over the mascarpone and fruit and bake in the oven at gas mark 6, 200°C (400°F) for 20 minutes. The filling will bubble through the cobbler.

11ᵗʰ August

SUMMER PUDDING WITH NECTARINES
Serves 6

1 brioche loaf, sliced with crusts removed
450g, 1lb blackcurrants
225g, 8oz whitecurrants
175g, 6oz caster sugar
6 nectarines

Use the brioche slices to line the bottom and sides of a 1.2 litre, 2 pint pudding basin. Reserve a couple of slices for the top. Put the black and whitecurrants in a saucepan with the sugar and cook gently until the juices run. Peel and dice the nectarines and add to the currants. Simmer for a few more minutes and then pour onto the brioche slices. Reserve any left over fruit and juice. Top with brioche slices to enclose the fruit. Cover with a plate and put a weight on top. Chill overnight. When you are ready to serve it turn the pudding out and cover any brioche slices not coloured with juice with the remaining fruit and juice.

12ᵗʰ August

CHERRY AND REDCURRANT
UPSIDE DOWN CAKE
Serves 6

225g, 8oz cherries, halved and stoned
100g, 4oz redcurrants
75g, 3oz caster sugar
75g, 3oz butter
75g, 3oz soft brown sugar
3 eggs
150g, 5oz self-raising flour, sieved
few drops of vanilla essence

Arrange the cherries and redcurrants over the base of a greased 20cm, 8in cake tin. Sprinkle the caster sugar over them. Cream together the butter and brown sugar and gradually add the eggs alternately with the flour. Beat in the vanilla essence. Pour the mixture over the fruit and smooth the top. Bake in the oven at gas mark 4, 180°C (350°F) for 30 minutes or until a skewer stuck in the middle comes out clean. Invert the pudding onto a plate and serve with cream.

13ᵗʰ August

Loganberries are in season now - they are similar to raspberries but more of a dull red. They are rather sour when raw so need to be sweetened.

LOGANBERRY MERINGUE ICE CREAM PUDDING
Serves 8

50g, 2oz light muscovado sugar
2 tbsp cocoa, sifted
600ml, 1pt double cream, whipped
8 meringues, crushed
450g, 1lb loganberries

Stir the sugar and cocoa into the cream along with the crushed meringues. Cut up the loganberries and fold them in. Spoon the mixture into a freezer container and smooth the top. Cover and freeze for about 4 hours. An hour before serving, transfer to the fridge. Turn out of the freezer container and serve.

14*th* August

These are delicious little puddings, made in ramekins suitable for a family supper or for a supper party. You could use raspberries and peaches instead of the tayberries and nectarines.

TAYBERRY AND NECTARINE TOFFEE PUDDINGS
Serves 4

4 nectarines, stoned
50g, 2oz butter
50g, 2oz caster sugar
2 tbsp double cream
100g, 4oz tayberries
50g, 2oz brown breadcrumbs
25g, 1oz brown sugar
15g, ½oz plain flour
½ tsp mixed spice

Cut the nectarines into small chunks. Place the butter, sugar and cream into a small saucepan and heat gently until the butter is melted and the sugar dissolved. Spoon half this mixture into the base of 4 ramekin dishes and top with the chopped nectarines and some tayberries. Mix together the breadcrumbs, brown sugar, flour and mixed spice. Spoon some over the fruit. Lay the rest of the nectarines and tayberries over the breadcrumb mixture and drizzle over the rest of the buttery mixture. Bake in a preheated oven at gas mark 4, 180°C (350°F) for 30 minutes. Cool slightly before serving with whipped cream.

15th August

India gained independence on 15th August 1947. Here is an Indian sweet, popular in India and in Indian restaurants in Britain.

GULAB JAMUN
Makes 24

225g, 8oz dried milk
1 tbsp plain flour
1 tbsp baking powder
150ml, ¼pt milk
oil for deep frying
225g, 8oz granulated sugar
300ml, ½pt water
2tbsp rosewater

Sieve together the dried milk, flour and baking powder. Add enough milk to make a stiff dough and leave to stand for at least 30 minutes. Roll the dough into walnut-sized balls. Heat the oil in a deep frying pan and fry the balls until they puff up and are golden brown. Don't allow the oil to get too hot. Drain on some kitchen paper. Make a syrup by dissolving the sugar in the water and bringing it to the boil. Boil for 2 to 3 minutes. Then add the rosewater. Put the cooked balls in a glass bowl and pour the hot syrup over them. Leave for a few hours before serving.

16th August

Save the egg whites for tomorrow's Loganberry Snow.

APRICOT ICE CREAM
Serves 4 – 6

75g, 3oz granulated sugar
3 egg yolks
675g, 1½lb apricots, stoned and puréed and sieved

75g, 3oz icing sugar
juice of 1 lemon
300ml, ½pt double cream

Put the sugar and 120ml, 4fl oz of water in a saucepan and bring to the boil. Boil for 3 minutes. In the meantime whisk the egg yolks until thick and then slowly pour on the sugar syrup while continuing to whisk. Sprinkle the icing sugar onto the apricot purée and add the lemon juice – stir to combine. Fold into the egg yolk mixture. Lastly whip the cream until thick and fold it into the apricot and egg mixture. Pour into a freezer container and freeze until firm.

17ᵗʰ August

LOGANBERRY SNOW
Serves 4

350g, 12oz loganberries
1 tbsp rosewater
50g, 2oz caster sugar
175g, 6oz cream cheese
2 egg whites (from yesterday)
50g, 2oz icing sugar

Cook the loganberries in a little water until they soften. Purée and sieve them. Add the rosewater. Cool and then freeze the puréed loganberries until the slushy stage. Beat the sugar and cream cheese together and beat into the half frozen loganberries. Freeze until just firm. When you are ready to serve the pudding, whisk the egg whites with the icing sugar and fold into the loganberry mixture to give a swirled effect.

18ᵗʰ August

CHOCOLATE POTS
Serves 6 – 8

175g, 6oz good plain chocolate
4 tbsp water
15g, ½oz butter
1 tsp vanilla essence
3 eggs, separated

Melt the chocolate with the water and butter and stir until smooth. Add the vanilla essence and stir in the egg yolks. Lastly whisk the egg whites until stiff and stir into the chocolate mixture. When all the egg white is well incorporated pour into ramekin dishes and chill overnight.

19ᵗʰ August

This is delicious with Blackcurrant Kissel (see page 144).

REDCURRANT BAVAROIS
Serves 4 – 6

300ml, ½pt milk
3 egg yolks (save 2 whites for tomorrow's sorbet)
65g, 2½oz caster sugar
1 sachet of gelatine + 3 tbsp water
few drops of vanilla essence
350g, 12oz redcurrants, puréed and sieved
300ml, ½pt double cream

Heat the milk until nearly boiling. Beat the egg yolks and sugar until light and creamy. Pour the milk onto the egg yolks, mix well and heat gently, stirring until the custard thickens. Soften the gelatine in the water and heat gently over a pan of hot water to dissolve it. Add to the custard and strain. Add the vanilla essence. Leave to cool and then stir in the redcurrant purée. Chill until nearly set, then fold in the whipped cream. Pour into a charlotte mould and chill for at least 4 hours.

20ᵗʰ August

SUMMER FRUITS SORBET
Serves 4 - 6

225g, 8oz raspberries
100g, 4oz redcurrants
100g, 4oz blackcurrants
150g, 5oz caster sugar
Juice of ½ a lemon
2 tbsp framboise (raspberry liqueur)
2 egg whites

Pureé and sieve the fruits together. Stir in the caster sugar, lemon juice and framboise. Freeze until the slushy stage. Then take out of the freezer and beat the mixture. Whisk the egg whites and fold into the semi frozen sorbet. Return to the freezer and freeze until firm.

21ˢᵗ August

PEACH AND BLACKCURRANT SUMMER PIE
Serves 6 – 8

3 slices of white bread, crusts removed
450g, 1lb blackcurrants
3 peaches, peeled and sliced after plunging into boiling water
150g, 5oz caster sugar
225g, 8oz puff pastry
milk for brushing over the pastry and caster sugar for sprinkling

Line a 23cm, 9in flan dish with the bread, cutting it to shape. Mix the blackcurrants and sliced peaches with the sugar. Spread over the bread. Roll out the puff pastry into a circle and place on top of the fruit, pressing it down lightly at the edges. Make a couple of holes in the pastry to allow steam to escape. Brush with a little milk and dust with caster sugar. Cook in the oven at gas mark 5, 190°C (375°F) for 30 minutes. Serve with cream or vanilla ice cream.

22nd August

BLACKCURRANT AND APPLE WITH
HAZELNUT CRUMBLE
Serves 4 – 6

225g, 8oz blackcurrants
75g, 3oz granulated sugar
450g, 1lb cooking apples, peeled and cored
1 tbsp brown sugar

For the crumble
150g, 5oz plain flour
25g, 1oz hazelnuts
100g, 4oz butter
50g, 2oz caster sugar

Heat the blackcurrants with the sugar for a few minutes until the juices run and sieve them to produce a smooth purée. Slice the apples into an ovenproof dish and pour the purée on top. Sprinkle with the brown sugar. To make the crumble, put all the ingredients in a food processor and process until the mixture is crumbly. Spread over the top of the apple slices and blackcurrant purée. Bake in a preheated oven at gas mark 5, 190°C (375°F) for 30 minutes. Serve hot with cream.

23rd August

Save the egg whites for the Soufflés the day after tomorrow.

REDCURRANT AND HONEY ICE CREAM
Serves 6 – 8

450g, 1lb redcurrants
3 tbsp clear honey
75g, 3oz granulated sugar
120ml, 4 fl oz water

3 egg yolks
300ml, ½pt whipping cream

Purée the redcurrants and sieve them. Mix the honey into the redcurrant purée. Meanwhile dissolve the sugar in the water and boil for 5 minutes. Beat the egg yolks until thick. Pour the sugar syrup onto the egg yolks while continuing to whisk until you have a frothy, creamy mixture. Whip the cream and fold into the egg mixture along with the redcurrant purée. When everything is evenly blended pour into a freezer container and freeze for an hour. Take out and beat the mixture to help reduce ice crystals and beat again after another hour. Return to the freezer and freeze until firm.

24th August

This is St Bartholomew's day. St Bartholomew was the Patron Saint of butchers. St Bartholomew's Fair used to be held in Smithfield in London and traditionally apples dipped in honey were sold – these were the forerunners to toffee apples.

TOFFEE APPLES
Makes 8

8 short wooden skewers
8 good eating apples
325g, 12oz demerara sugar
40g, 1½oz butter
1 tsp white wine vinegar
90ml, 3fl oz water
1 tbsp golden syrup

Push a skewer into the core of each apple. Heat the sugar, butter, vinegar, water and syrup gently in a saucepan until the sugar has dissolved. Then boil for 5 minutes without stirring until a little mixture dropped into cold water forms a hard ball. Remove from the heat and dip the pan into cold water at once to stop the cooking. Dip the apples into the mixture and twirl around until evenly coated. Place on an oiled baking sheet until the toffee has hardened.

AUGUST

25ᵗʰ August

APPLE AND BLACKBERRY HOT SOUFFLÉS
Serves 6

300ml, ½pt apple and blackberry purée
75g, 3oz caster sugar
3 egg whites (from 23 Aug)

Butter six 150ml, ¼pt small pudding basins or mini soufflé dishes. Put a small spoonful of blackberry and apple purée in the bottom of each one. Whisk the egg whites until stiff and whisk in the caster sugar. Fold the purée into this meringue mixture until evenly combined. Spoon equal amounts into the pudding basins. Pop in the oven at gas mark 6, 200°C (400°F) on preheated baking sheets for 10 minutes. Serve immediately, dusted with icing sugar if liked.

26ᵗʰ August

RASPBERRY CREAM ICE WITH REDCURRANT RIPPLE
Serves 6

2 tbsp framboise (raspberry liqueur)
450g, 1lb raspberries, puréed and sieved
2 egg whites (use yolks tomorrow)
75g, 3oz caster sugar
300ml, ½pt double cream, whipped
175g, 6oz redcurrants
50g, 2oz granulated sugar

Stir the framboise into the raspberry purée. Beat the egg whites until stiff and beat in the caster sugar. Fold this meringue mixture into the double cream. Then fold in the raspberry purée. Pour into a freezer container and freeze for 2 or 3 hours. Meanwhile gently heat the redcurrants with a tablespoon of water and the sugar and simmer for a few minutes. Sieve the redcurrants and reserve the purée. Take the semi frozen raspberry cream out of the freezer and make 3 or 4 holes

160

along the centre. Pour the redcurrant juice into the holes and run a knife through the ice cream to give a marbled effect. Refreeze until firm.

27ᵗʰ August

APRICOT AND ALMOND TART
Serves 6

Shortcrust pastry (see page 5)
450g, 1lb apricots, peeled, halved and stoned
100g, 4oz butter
100g, 4oz caster sugar
100g, 4oz ground almonds
2 eggs + 2 egg yolks
175g, 6oz icing sugar
2 tbsp lemon juice

Roll out the pastry and line a greased 20cm, 8in flan tin. Arrange the apricot halves over the base. Beat together the butter, sugar, ground almonds, whole eggs and egg yolks. Spread the mixture over the apricots and cook in the oven at gas mark 4, 180°C (350°F) for 40 minutes until risen and golden brown. Mix the icing sugar and lemon juice together and spread over the tart when cooled. Allow to set before serving.

28ᵗʰ August

Save the egg yolks for tomorrow's trifle.

BAKED ALASKA
Serves 8

1 whisked sponge (see page 6)
100g, 4oz strawberries
100g, 4oz raspberries
450g, 1lb vanilla ice cream, slightly softened
2 egg whites
100g, 4oz caster sugar

Put the sponge base into a deep round baking dish and arrange the fruit on top. Spread the ice cream over the fruit and put in the freezer to keep frozen while you make the meringue topping. Whisk the egg whites until stiff and gradually add the caster sugar. Spoon the meringue over the ice cream and bake at once in a very hot oven for a few minutes, until the meringue is tinged brown. Serve immediately.

29ᵗʰ August

TAYBERRY AND AMARETTO TRIFLE
Serves 4

3 egg yolks (2 from yesterday)
75g, 3oz caster sugar
225g, 8oz mascarpone
2 tbsp Amaretto (almond flavoured liqueur)
1 egg white
450g, 1lb tayberries
175g, 6oz macaroons, crushed

Whisk the egg yolks and sugar together. Gradually whisk in the mascarpone and Amaretto. Whisk the egg white and fold into the mascarpone mixture. Make layers in a small serving bowl of tayberries, then some of the mascarpone mixture, then some of the crushed macaroons. Repeat the layers ending with the macaroons.

30ᵗʰ August

PEARS BELLE HÉLÈNE
Serves 4 – 6

Vanilla ice cream (see page 144)
6 pears, peeled, cored and halved

Chocolate fudge sauce
25g, 1oz plain chocolate
15g, ½oz butter
1 small can evaporated milk
50g, 2oz soft brown sugar
2 tbsp golden syrup

To make the sauce put all the ingredients in a saucepan and heat gently until melted. Bring to the boil, then lower the heat and simmer for 5 minutes by which time the sauce should be thick and glossy. Arrange the pears round the ice cream in a dish or on separate plates and pour over the chocolate sauce.

31ˢᵗ August

LOGANBERRY WATER ICE
Serves 4 – 6

100g, 4oz granulated sugar
150ml, ¼pt water
3 lemon-scented geranium leaves
450g, 1lb loganberries, sieved and puréed

Make a syrup by dissolving the sugar in the water over a gentle heat and then add the geranium leaves, bring to the boil and and boil for 5 minutes. Strain to remove the geranium leaves and when cool mix into the loganberry purée, pour into a freezer container and freeze, beating twice at hourly intervals.

1ˢᵗ September

Sir William Gage planted some French plum trees near Bury St Edmunds back in the 1700s – the plums turned out to be green and became known first as the green Gage's plum, which was then shortened to greengage. Greengages are in season late August to early September.

GREENGAGE TART
Serves 6

Pastry
175g, 6oz plain flour
75g, 3oz butter
25g, 1oz hazelnuts, roasted and chopped
1 tbsp light brown sugar

450g, 1lb greengages, halved and stoned
2 eggs
300ml, ½pt single cream
1 tbsp caster sugar

Make the pastry by rubbing the butter into the flour, adding the hazelnuts and sugar and binding together with a little water. Roll into a ball and then roll out and line a greased 20cm, 8in flan dish. Bake blind at gas mark 4, 180°C (350°F) for 10 minutes. Arrange the fruit cut side down over the pastry. Beat the eggs with the cream and the sugar. Pour over the fruit and return to the oven for 30 minutes.

2ⁿᵈ September

Mulberries ripen about this time of year and make a great pie filling if you are lucky enough to get your hands on some.

MULBERRRY PIE
Serves 6 – 8

Double quantity shortcrust pastry (see page 5)
5 sponge fingers, crumbled

450g, 1lb mulberries, hulled
75g, 3oz caster sugar

Roll out two circles of pastry, one bigger than the other. Use the bigger one to line a greased 23cm, 9in pie dish. Prick the bottom and bake in the oven at gas mark 4, 180°C (350°F) for 10 minutes. Sprinkle the sponge finger crumbs over the pastry (these help to absorb juices from the mulberries). Fill the pie with mulberries. Sprinkle over the sugar. Fit the other circle of pastry over the mulberries and press onto the base pastry around the edge. Sprinkle the top with more sugar and return to the oven for 30 minutes until the pastry is brown and crisp. Serve with single cream.

3rd September

PEARS WITH REDCURRANT SORBET
Serves 4

75g, 3oz granulated sugar
60ml, 2fl oz water
450g, 1lb pears, peeled, cored and sliced

For the sorbet
450g, 1lb redcurrants
225g, 8oz granulated sugar
juice of 1 small lemon
1 egg white

Make up a sugar syrup by combining the sugar and water. Heat gently until the sugar has dissolved. Add the sliced pears and simmer for 20 minutes to soften the pears. To make the sorbet, heat the redcurrants in a little water until the juices run. Sieve to remove the pips and make up to 600ml, 1 pint with a little water if necessary. Heat the redcurrant juice with the sugar to dissolve the sugar and then simmer for 5 minutes. Leave to cool, covering with a lid to stop a skin forming. Transfer to a freezer container and freeze until slushy. Take out and whisk the mixture. Beat the egg white and gently fold it in. Return to the freezer and freeze until firm. Serve each person with a portion of poached pears and a dollop of redcurrant sorbet.

4ᵗʰ September

Save the egg yolks, one for the Clafoutis tomorrow and one for the Paris-Brest the following day.

BLACKBERRY SNOW
Serves 4

450g, 1lb blackberries
2 egg whites
100g, 4oz caster sugar
300ml, ½pt double cream, whipped

Rub the blackberries through a sieve to form a purée, pour into a container and freeze for 2 hours. Whisk the egg whites until stiff and gradually add the sugar while continuing to whisk. Take the blackberry purée from the freezer and mash to break down any large ice crystals. Fold the cream and egg white mixture together and fold into the semi-frozen blackberry purée to give a swirled effect. Spoon into glasses or into a serving bowl and serve immediately.

5ᵗʰ September
CHERRY CLAFOUTIS
Serves 4 – 6

75g, 3oz plain flour
2eggs + 1 egg yolk (from yesterday)
300ml, ½pt milk
350g, 12oz black cherries, stoned
50g, 2oz brown sugar

Sift the flour into a bowl, make a well in the centre and drop in the eggs and extra egg yolk. Beat and then add the milk and mix until smooth. Leave to stand for 30 minutes. In a baking tin heat a spoonful of oil until it is really hot. Pour in the batter mixture and lay the cherries on top. Sprinkle with the brown sugar and put in a preheated oven at gas mark 7, 220°C (425°F) for about 20 minutes and then lower the heat to gas mark 5, 190°C (375°F) and cook for another 10 minutes. Serve warm with extra sugar if necessary and single cream.

6ᵗʰ September

Paris-Brest is a ring-shaped choux pastry, filled with cream and sprinkled with almonds and powdered sugar. It was created in 1891 by a Parisian pastry cook whose pâtisserie was situated along the route of the bicycle race from Paris to Brest. His idea was to bake his éclairs in the shape of bicycle wheels in honour of all the cyclists. The first race took place on 6ᵗʰ September 1891. The Paris Brest Paris (PBP) is the oldest bicycling event that is still regularly run – riders cover 750 miles. It was a race for professional cyclists in its early years, but is now a non-competitive endurance challenge.

PARIS-BREST
Serves 4 – 6

25g, 1oz butter
1 tsp caster sugar
150ml, ¼pt milk
100g, 4oz plain flour
2 eggs + one extra egg yolk (from 4 Sept)
300ml, ½pt double cream
2 tbsp icing sugar + extra for sprinkling
25g, 1oz flaked almonds

Put the butter, caster sugar and milk into a saucepan and bring slowly to the boil. Turn off the heat and stir in the sifted flour, beating well with a wooden spoon. Beat two eggs into the mixture and the extra yolk. Pipe or spoon the choux pastry into a ring on a greased baking sheet and bake in the oven at gas mark 5, 190°C (375°F) for 30 minutes in a hot oven until browned. Cool the choux pastry and then split in half. For the cream filling whip the cream with the icing sugar and spoon onto the bottom half of the ring. Put the top half on and sprinkle with the flaked almonds and rest of the icing sugar.

7ᵗʰ September

BRAMBLE MOUSSE
Serves 6 – 8

450g, 1lb blackberries
juice of 1 lemon
3 eggs, separated
175g, 6oz caster sugar
2 sachets of gelatine
300ml, ½pt double cream, whipped

Cook the blackberries in the lemon juice in a saucepan with a tightly fitting lid. When the blackberries have softened, remove from the heat, sieve them and allow to cool. Put 3 tablespoons of water in a small saucepan and sprinkle in the gelatine. Leave to soften a little and then heat very gently until the gelatine has dissolved. Leave to cool. Whisk the egg yolks and gradually add the caster sugar, whisking until you have a thick, pale mixture. Stir in the cooled blackberry mixture and the gelatine. Add the whipped cream and lastly whisk the egg whites until stiff and fold them in too. Pour the mousse into a bowl and leave to set.

8ᵗʰ September

George III married Charlotte Sophia of Mecklenburg Strelitz on this day in 1761. Their coronation took place on 22ⁿᵈ September of the same year. Apple Charlotte came into existence at some point after that, probably named after Queen Charlotte, said to be patron of apple growers.

APPLE CHARLOTTE
Serves 4 – 6

675g, 1½lb cooking apples, peeled, cored and sliced
grated rind and juice of 1 lemon
½ tsp ground cinnamon

100g, 4oz caster sugar
50g, 2oz melted butter
enough thin slices of brown or white bread to line your dish
(crusts removed)

Cook the apples with the rind and juice of the lemon, cinnamon and 2 tablespoons of water until tender. Remove from the heat and mix in the sugar beating well. Meanwhile brush the melted butter all over the slices of bread and use them to line a 1.2 litre, 2pt soufflé dish, overlapping them if you like. Pour in the apple purée. Fit more bread over the top to cover the apple and bake in a reasonably hot oven at gas mark 6, 200°C (400°F) for about 30 minutes.

9ᵗʰ September

MULBERRY AND PEAR UPSIDE DOWN PUDDING
Serves 4 – 6

100g, 4oz golden syrup
100g, 4oz mulberries
3 pears, peeled, cored and sliced
grated rind of 1 lemon

For the cake
100g, 4oz butter
100g, 4oz brown sugar
100g, 4oz self-raising flour
2 eggs
2 tbsp milk

Spoon the golden syrup into the base of a lightly greased 20cm, 8in deep round cake tin. Arrange the mulberries and pear slices over the golden syrup and scatter the lemon rind on as well. To make the sponge beat together all the ingredients and spoon over the fruit. Bake in the oven at gas mark 4, 180°C (350°F) for 35 minutes and cool in the tin a little before turning out so that the mulberries and pears are on top. Serve warm with cream.

10th September

The blueberries give the inside of this pudding great colour. The apples melt into the purple fruit.

APPLE AND BLUEBERRY WALNUT CRISP
Serves 4 - 6

350g, 12oz blueberries
350g, 12oz cooking apples, peeled, cored and sliced
juice and grated rind of 1 lemon
175g, 6oz light brown sugar

For the topping
175g, 6oz plain flour
1 tsp baking powder
100g, 4oz granulated sugar
50g, 2oz butter
1 large egg, beaten
a handful of walnuts, chopped
½ tsp ground cinnamon

Mix the blueberries and apples with the lemon rind, juice and the brown sugar and put in a round 20cm, 8in ovenproof dish. To make the topping, mix together the flour, baking powder and sugar. Rub in the butter, then add the egg and nuts. Spread this mixture over the fruit. Sprinkle the cinnamon over the top. Cook in a preheated oven at gas mark 6, 200°C (400°F) for 30 minutes. The top should be nicely browned. Serve with cream or crème fraîche.

11ᵗʰ September

PEAR AND REDCURRANT COBBLER
Serves 4

½ tsp ground cinnamon
¼ tsp ground nutmeg
1 tsp cornflour
150ml, ¼pt water
225g, 8oz redcurrants
50g, 2oz granulated sugar
3 large pears, peeled, cored and sliced

For the cobbler
175g, 6oz wholemeal flour
1 tsp baking powder
50g, 2oz caster sugar
40g, 1½oz melted butter
1 egg
150ml, ¼pt soured cream

Mix the spices and cornflour and gradually add the water to make a smooth paste. Put the redcurrants and granulated sugar in a saucepan, add the liquid paste and bring gradually to the boil and simmer for 3 minutes. Put the pears in an ovenproof dish and pour over the redcurrant mixture. Meanwhile mix the flour, baking powder and caster sugar in a bowl. Add the melted butter, egg and soured cream and mix together. Drop spoonfuls of this mixture over the pears and redcurrants until they are almost entirely covered. Bake in the oven at gas mark 5, 190°C (375°F) for 30 minutes. Serve hot with cream.

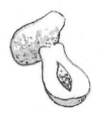

12ᵗʰ September

If you grow autumn cropping raspberries such as Autumn Bliss, this sorbet is an ideal way to make use of them. It is delicious and the framboise enhances the flavour of the raspberries.

RASPBERRY SORBET
Serves 4

juice of ½ a lemon
75g, 3oz caster sugar
1 tbsp framboise (raspberry liqueur)
350g, 12oz raspberries, puréed and sieved
2 egg whites

Add the lemon juice, sugar and framboise to the puréed and sieved raspberries and mix well. Pour into a freezer container and freeze until the slushy stage. Remove from the freezer and beat well. Whisk the egg whites and fold them into the half frozen mixture. Return to the freezer and freeze until you are ready to serve it.

13ᵗʰ September

BLACKBERRY AND APPLE AMBER
Serves 6

Shortcrust pastry (see page 5)
450g, 1lb cooking apples, peeled, cored and chopped
100g, 4oz blackberries
juice of 1 lemon
100g, 4oz brown sugar
2 eggs, separated
100g, 4oz caster sugar

Roll out the pastry and use to line a greased 20cm, 8in flan dish. Prick and bake blind in the oven at gas mark 5, 190°C (375°F) for 15 minutes. Cook the apples and blackberries with the lemon juice and brown sugar over a gentle heat for 15 minutes. Sieve the apple and blackberry mixture and when slightly cooled mix in the egg yolks. Spread over the pastry base. Whisk the egg whites until stiff and whisk in the sugar bit by bit until the meringue is thick and glossy. Spread over the blackberry and apple. Bake in the oven at gas mark 3, 160°C (325°F) for a further 40 minutes, by which time the meringue will be golden and crisp on top but soft inside. Serve with single cream.

14th September

PLUM AND PORT PARFAIT
Serves 4

450g, 1lb plums
2 wine glasses of port
1 tbsp granulated sugar
2 tsp ground cinnamon
3 eggs, separated
75g, 3oz caster sugar
300ml, ½pt double cream

Cook the plums in a saucepan with half the port and the granulated sugar until the plums are soft. Remove the stones and purée the plums together with the cinnamon. Leave to cool. Whisk the egg yolks and add the caster sugar, whisking until they are very pale and thick. Fold into the purée. Whip the cream with the rest of the port and fold into the plum mixture. Whisk the egg whites until stiff and fold them in. Pour into a container and freeze until firm.

15th September

Pear Day at Cannon Hall Museum in Barnsley, Yorkshire takes place around this time of year.

CHOCOLATE AND PEAR MERINGUE PIE
Serves 4 - 6

Pastry
100g, 4oz plain flour
25g, 1oz cocoa powder
75g, 3oz butter
1 egg yolk

Filling
3 ripe pears, peeled, cored and quartered
2 egg whites
100g, 4oz caster sugar
2 tbsp cocoa powder

To make the pastry, mix together the flour and cocoa powder, rub in the butter and mix to a dough with a little cold water. Roll out the pastry and use to line a greased 20cm, 8in flan case. Chill for 30 minutes. Prick the pastry and bake the flan blind in the oven at gas mark 5, 190°C (375°F) for 10 minutes. Arrange the pear quarters over the flan. Whisk the egg whites until stiff and then whisk in the sugar. Fold in the cocoa powder and spoon the mixture over the pears. Bake in the oven at gas mark 5, 190°C (375°F) for 30 minutes. Serve warm with cream or Greek yoghurt.

16ᵗʰ September

Use yesterday's left over egg yolk and today's 2 egg yolks for tomorrow's blackberry ice cream.

PLUM AND BRAMBLE FOOL
Serves 6 – 8

900g, 2lb plums
100g, 4oz granulated sugar
150ml, ¼pt double cream, whipped
150ml, ¼pt mascarpone
2 egg whites
100g, 4oz blackberries, sieved

Cook the plums with the granulated sugar in a little water for 10 minutes. Discard the stones and purée the flesh. Mix with the whipped cream and mascarpone. Whisk the egg whites until fairly stiff and fold into the mixture. Divide between individual dishes and swirl a little of the sieved blackberries over each dish.

17ᵗʰ September

BLACKBERRY ICE CREAM
Serves 4 – 6

450g, 1lb blackberries, puréed and sieved
75g, 3oz icing sugar
squeeze of lemon juice
75g, 3oz granulated sugar + 120ml, 4 fl oz water
3 egg yolks (from 15 & 16 Sept)
300ml, ½pt double cream, whipped

Put the blackberry purée in a bowl with the icing sugar and a squeeze of lemon juice. Dissolve the sugar with the water in a heavy-based saucepan and boil for 5 minutes. Whisk the egg yolks until thick and then whisk in the boiling syrup. Continue to whisk until the mixture cools and thickens again. Fold in the blackberry purée and cream. Spoon into a freezer container and freeze until firm.

18ᵗʰ September

The Barnstaple Fair is an annual event held over 4 days and always starts on the Wednesday preceding 20ᵗʰ September. The pear orchards of Devon used to supply the stalls at the Fair and this is a traditional dish.

BARNSTAPLE FAIR PEARS
Serves 4

4 large Comice pears
25g, 1oz flaked almonds
50g, 2oz caster sugar
300ml, ½pt red wine
2 cloves

Peel the pears but leave the stalks on. Push the flaked almonds into the pear flesh. Put the sugar, wine and cloves in a saucepan and heat gently until the sugar has dissolved. Add the pears, standing them upright and simmer gently for 15 minutes, basting every so often. Transfer the pears to a serving dish. Boil the remaining syrup fast to reduce by half. Pour over the pears and serve hot or cold. The pears will have turned a temptingly luscious deep red.

19th September

In America National Butterscotch Pudding Day is celebrated on this day. If you like butterscotch, like me, your mouth may already be watering. Like all food related special days it's a good excuse to get cooking.

BUTTERSCOTCH PUDDING
Serves 4 – 6

For the sponge
100g, 4oz light muscovado sugar
100g, 4oz butter
2 eggs
4 tbsp milk
175g, 6oz self-raising flour
1 tsp baking powder

Topping
75g, 3oz butter
100g, 4oz light muscovado sugar
4 tbsp double cream

Combine all the ingredients for the sponge and beat until smooth. Grease a 25 x 17.5cm, 10 x 7in rectangular ovenproof dish and spread the sponge evenly out in the dish. Bake for about 40 minutes in the oven at gas mark 4, 180°C (350°F). To prepare the sauce melt the butter, add the sugar and cream and bring to the boil. Simmer for a few minutes stirring every so often. Pour the sauce over the sponge and put under the grill for a couple of minutes. The sauce will begin to bubble. Serve immediately with cream or crème fraîche.

20th September

Oktoberfest is a two week festival, held in Munich in Bavaria. Oktoberfest celebrations are also held around the world. So, if you can't get to the Fair in Germany, you can participate in a local event. It's time to eat, drink, and be merry! Each year, the Oktoberfest is opened as the Mayor of Munich taps a keg of beer and celebrated with lots of food, music, dancing, rides, and carnival booths. The very first Oktoberfest was held on October 12, 1810. It was held to commemorate the marriage of Crown Prince Ludwig (King Ludwig I) to Princess Therese of Sachsen-Hildburghausen. The marriage was celebrated annually, and came to be known as Oktoberfest. Celebrations were eventually moved to September, as the weather was better. The date varies slightly from year to year. Here is a Bavarian Strudel, a traditional German pudding.

BAVARIAN STRUDEL
Serves 4 - 6

Pastry
100g, 4oz butter
175g, 6oz plain flour
50g, 2oz caster sugar
3 tbsp milk

Filling
675g, 1½lb apples, peeled, cored and sliced
25g, 1oz sultanas
½ tsp mixed spice
75g, 3oz caster sugar
a handful of breadcrumbs
milk and sugar for glazing

Rub the butter into the flour. Add sugar and bind with milk. Knead a little to make a smooth dough. Mix the sliced apples with sultanas, spice and sugar. Add a handful of breadcrumbs. Roll out the pastry on a floured surface into a long strip. Put the apple mixture down the middle. Fold over the sides of the pastry and roll up. Brush over with milk and dust with sugar. Bake in the oven at gas mark 4, 180°C (350°F) for 30 minutes.

21ˢᵗ September

PEAR AND BLACKBERRY SPONGE PUDDING
Serves 4 - 6

Sponge base
100g, 4oz butter
50g, 2oz caster sugar
50g, 2oz self-raising flour
50g, 2oz wholemeal self-raising flour
1 egg

Topping
450g, 1lb pears, peeled, cored and halved
100g, 4oz blackberries
150ml, ¼pt soured cream
1 egg
½ tsp vanilla essence
50g, 2oz golden caster sugar

Combine all the ingredients for the sponge together in a food processor and process until blended. Spoon into the base of a greased 20cm, 8in square cake tin. Arrange the halved pears and blackberries over the sponge. Beat the cream, egg, vanilla essence and sugar together and pour over the top. Bake in the oven at gas mark 5, 190°C (375°F) for about 30 minutes. The topping will set as the pudding cools.

22ⁿᵈ September

The autumn equinox falls usually on 22ⁿᵈ or 23ʳᵈ September so here is an aptly named Autumn Pudding. This is delicious and a change from the more usual summer pudding.

AUTUMN PUDDING
Serves 4 - 6

225g, 8oz cooking apples, peeled, cored and sliced
225g, 8oz blackberries
225g, 8oz plums, halved and de-stoned
175g, 6oz granulated sugar
10 slices of white bread, crusts removed

Cook the apples, plums and blackberries together with the sugar and 4 tablespoons of water until tender. Line the bottom and sides of a 1.2litre, 2pt pudding basin with the bread. Reserve a little of the juice from the fruit. Pour the stewed fruit into the basin and top with a slice of bread to make a lid. Put a plate on top of the basin and weight it down. Chill the pudding overnight. Turn out onto a serving dish. Pour the reserved juice over the top to conceal any white bits of bread.

23ʳᵈ September

DATE, WALNUT AND FIG TOFFEE TART
Serves 6 – 8

Shortcrust pastry (see page 5)
175g, 6oz granulated sugar + 2 tbsp water
175g, 6oz tin of evaporated milk
50g, 2oz butter
90ml, 3fl oz double cream
225g, 8oz dates
5 dried figs
50g, 2oz walnuts

Roll out the pastry and use to line a greased 23cm, 9in flan tin. Bake blind in the oven at gas mark 4, 180°C (350°F) for 10 minutes. In the meantime make the toffee. Put the sugar in a saucepan with the water and boil until a caramel colour. Pour on the evaporated milk – be careful, the mixture will froth up – then stir in the butter and cream. Stir over a low heat until the sauce is smooth and the caramel melted. Allow to cool. Spread the dates and figs and walnuts evenly over the pastry and spoon the toffee sauce over the fruit. Leave to set before serving.

24ᵗʰ September

The apples blend well with the blackcurrants and make this ice cream less strong than a pure blackcurrant one. My children love it.

APPLE AND BLACKCURRANT ICE CREAM
Serves 8

225g, 8oz cooking apples, peeled, cored and chopped
225g, 8oz blackcurrants
2 tbsp granulated sugar
4 tbsp water
4 eggs, separated
100g, 4oz caster sugar
300ml, ½pt cream, whipped

Combine the apples, blackcurrants, granulated sugar and water and simmer for 15 minutes. Sieve the fruit to remove the blackcurrant pips. Whisk the egg whites and whisk in the caster sugar. Whisk the egg yolks until thick and creamy. Fold the fruit purée into the whipped cream and fold in the egg yolks. Lastly fold in the egg whites. Pour into a freezer container and freeze until firm.

25th September

TOFFEE WALNUT TART
Serves 4 - 6

Shortcrust pastry (see page 5)
225g, 8oz walnuts, roughly chopped
4 eggs, beaten
4 tbsp golden syrup
75g, 3oz butter
100g, 4oz brown sugar

Roll out the pastry and line a greased 20cm, 8in flan dish. Prick and bake blind in the oven at gas mark 4, 180°C (350°F) for 15 minutes. Leave to cool. Scatter the walnuts over the base. Put the eggs, golden syrup, butter and brown sugar in a bowl and place over a pan of simmering water. Stir, allowing the butter to melt and when evenly combined pour over the nuts. Bake in the oven at gas mark 4, 180°C (350°F) for about 25 minutes or until the filling is just set.

26th September

APPLE COBBLER
Serves 4 – 6

450g, 1lb cooking apples, peeled, cored and sliced
50g, 2oz brown sugar
1 tbsp orange juice
50g, 2oz stoned dates
2 bananas, sliced
1 tsp lemon juice

For the cobbler
225g, 8oz plain flour
¼ tsp ground ginger
1 tsp bicarbonate of soda
1 tsp cream of tartar

50g, 2oz butter
150ml, ¼pt milk
2 tbsp demerara sugar

Arrange the apples in an ovenproof dish, sprinkle with the sugar and pour on the orange juice. Stir in the dates and cover the fruit with the bananas tossed in lemon juice. To make the topping sift together the flour, ginger, bicarbonate of soda and cream of tartar and rub in the butter until the mixture resembles breadcrumbs. Pour the milk into the dry ingredients, mix to a dough and knead until smooth. Roll the dough into a circle to cover the apple mixture. Brush with milk and sprinkle with demerara sugar. Bake in the oven at gas mark 6, 200°C (400°F) for 20 minutes until the topping is well risen.

27th September

MAPLE AND WALNUT PRALINE ICE CREAM
Serves 4 - 6

For the praline
100g, 4oz granulated sugar
50g, 2oz walnuts

4 eggs, separated
150ml, ¼pt maple syrup
300ml, ½pt double cream, whipped

To make the praline put the sugar and walnuts in a heavy based pan and heat until the sugar turns to liquid. Do not stir but tilt the pan backwards and forwards to distribute the sugar evenly. Remove from the heat and pour the mixture on to a greased baking tin to harden. Crush to a powder with a rolling pin. Whisk the egg yolks with warmed maple syrup until thick. Stir into the cream. Whisk the egg whites and fold in with the praline. Pour into a freezer container and freeze until firm.

28th September

Traditionally this is the last day one should pick and eat blackberries. Folklore tells us it is unlucky to eat them after Michaelmas Day on 29th September.

APPLE AND BLACKBERRY WITH
SHORTBREAD CRUMBLE
Serves 6

450g, 1lb cooking apples, peeled, cored and sliced
225g, 8oz blackberries
100g, 4oz granulated sugar
2 tbsp water

Crumble
175g, 6oz plain flour
75g, 3oz butter
50g, 2oz granulated sugar

Put the sliced apples in a pie dish with the blackberries, caster sugar and water. Put the flour in a bowl. Add the butter and rub with the fingertips until the mixture resembles breadcrumbs. Stir in the caster sugar. Pile the crumble mixture on top of the fruit and press down gently. Bake in a preheated oven at gas mark 4, 180°C (350°F) for 30 to 40 minutes or until the crumble topping is golden brown.

29th September

WALNUT AND APPLE TART
Serves 6 - 8

Shortcrust pastry (see page 5)
450g, 1lb cooking apples, peeled and cored
150ml, ¼pt whipping cream
100g, 4oz caster sugar
1 egg

75g, 3oz plain flour
1 tsp vanilla essence
1 tsp ground cinnamon
¼ tsp ground nutmeg
75g, 3oz walnuts, chopped

Line a greased 23cm, 9in flan dish with the pastry. Slice the apples and transfer to the flan dish. Mix together the cream, sugar, egg, flour, vanilla essence and spices (this can be done in a food processor if you have one). Pour over apple slices and top with the walnuts. Bake at gas mark 4, 180°C (350°F) for 40 minutes. Serve warm.

30ᵗʰ September

APPLE BUTTERSCOTCH MERINGUE PIE
Serves 6 – 8

Shortcrust pastry (see page 5)
5 eating apples, peeled and cored
3 eggs
2 tbsp single cream
75g, 3oz demerara sugar
2 tbsp plain flour
100g, 4oz granulated sugar

Roll out the pastry and line a greased 20cm, 8in flan dish. Thinly slice the apples and fill the case. Beat together one whole egg, 2 egg yolks and the single cream. Mix this with the demerara sugar and flour. Spread this mixture over the apples and bake in the oven at gas mark 4, 180°C (350°F) for 30 minutes or until the apples are soft. Make the meringue topping by beating the 2 egg whites until stiff. Add the sugar gradually, beating constantly until the mixture is thick. Spoon the meringue over the filling. Swirl into peaks with a fork. Bake for a further 20 minutes until the meringue is lightly golden. Serve cold.

1ˢᵗ October

TARTE TATIN
Serves 4 – 6

Sweet shortcrust pastry (see page 5)
75g, 3oz butter
175g, 6oz muscovado or brown sugar
450g, 1lb cooking apples, peeled, cored and sliced
1 egg, beaten

Spread half the butter on the base of a round 20cm, 8in pie dish. Sprinkle all over with half the sugar. Lay the slices of apple neatly over the sugary base. Melt the remaining butter and pour over the fruit and sprinkle with remaining sugar. Roll out the pastry and cover the pie. Tuck the edges down between the apples and the edge of the dish. Brush with beaten egg. Put in the oven at gas mark 6, 200°C (400°F) for 30 minutes. Turn the tart upside down onto a serving dish. The apples will look caramelised.

2ⁿᵈ October

REDCURRANT AND APPLE STRUDEL
Serves 4 - 6

225g, 8oz puff pastry
4 large cooking apples, peeled, cored and sliced
2 tbsp soft brown sugar
1 tsp vanilla essence
100g, 4oz butter
4 tbsp breadcrumbs
2 tbsp redcurrant jelly
50g, 2oz chopped almonds
1 tsp icing sugar

Roll the pastry as thinly as possible on a well floured surface into a rectangle. Sprinkle the apple slices with brown sugar and the vanilla essence. Melt 50g, 2oz of the butter in a pan and fry the breadcrumbs until golden. Melt the rest of the butter and spread over the pastry. Sprinkle the breadcrumbs over the pastry, spreading the apples over the top. Dot with the redcurrant jelly and the almonds. Fold in the edges of the pastry and roll up like a Swiss roll. Place the strudel on a buttered baking tin and brush again with melted butter. Bake in the oven at gas mark 4, 180°C (375°F) for about 45 minutes, brushing with butter every so often. Dust with icing sugar and before serving.

3rd October

This is a flourless cake, delicious with Greek yoghurt or cream and you can eat it warm or cold.

CHOCOLATE AND HAZELNUT PUDDING
Serves 6

175g, 6oz plain chocolate
100g, 4oz butter
3 eggs, separated
100g, 4oz light brown sugar
100g, 4oz hazelnuts, ground

Melt the chocolate and butter together and stir until smooth. Whisk together the egg yolks and brown sugar until thick and creamy. Stir in the chocolate mixture and fold in the hazelnuts. Whisk the egg whites and carefully fold them in. Spoon into a greased 20cm, 8in deep flan dish and bake in the oven at gas mark 4, 180°C (350°F) for about 40 minutes or until a skewer stuck in the centre comes out clean.

4ᵗʰ October

APPLE AND FIG CRUMBLE
Serves 4 - 6

Filling
100g, 4oz figs, halved
150ml, ¼pt water
675g, 1½lb cooking apples, peeled, cored and chopped
75g, 3oz granulated sugar

Crumble
50g, 2oz plain flour
50g, 2oz porridge oats
50g, 2oz ground almonds
75g, 3oz butter
50g, 2oz brown sugar

Put the figs in a saucepan with the water and simmer for 5 minutes.
Mix with the apples and granulated sugar in a baking dish and pour
over the remaining liquid. Put the flour and oats in a bowl with the
ground almonds. Add the butter and rub with the fingertips until the
mixture resembles breadcrumbs. Stir in the brown sugar. Spread this
crumble mixture over the apples and figs and cook in the oven at gas
mark 4, 180°C (350°F) for 30 minutes.

5ᵗʰ October

These fritters are quick and easy and the children will love them.

APPLE FRITTERS
Makes about 12 fritters

75g, 3oz plain flour
pinch of salt
1 egg, separated

1 tbsp oil
2 tbsp milk
2 tbsp water
3 medium cooking apples, peeled, cored and cut into rings
oil for frying
caster sugar

Sift the flour and salt and make a well in the centre. Drop the egg yolk into this. Add the oil and gradually pour in the milk and water stirring the dry ingredients into the egg and liquid. Cover and leave for at least 30 minutes. Whisk the egg white until stiff and fold into the batter. Dust the apple rings with flour as this helps the batter to cling to them, coat with the batter and fry in batches for about five minutes, turning once. Dry on kitchen paper, sprinkle with caster sugar and serve.

6th October

PEACH AND HAZELNUT ICE CREAM
Serves 4

4 peaches
4 tbsp honey
3 egg yolks (use 2 whites tomorrow)
150ml, ¼pt double cream, whipped
50g, 2oz chopped hazelnuts
few drops of lemon juice

Peel the peaches, remove the stones and purée the flesh. Put the honey and 1 tablespoon of water in a saucepan and heat gently to melt the honey. Then bring to boiling point. Whisk the egg yolks and pour the hot syrup in a steady stream onto the egg yolks whisking all the time. Over a pan of simmering water continue to whisk until the mixture thickens. Whisk the peach purée and hazelnuts into the egg yolk mixture. Fold in the cream and add a little lemon juice. Pour into a freezer container and freeze until firm.

189

7ᵗʰ October

DAMSON SYLLABUB
Serves 4

450g, 1lb damsons, halved and stoned
100g, 4oz caster sugar
150ml, ¼pt water
2 tbsp brandy
2 egg whites (from yesterday)
300ml, ½pt double cream, whipped

Place the damsons in a saucepan with the sugar and water. Heat gently and simmer until soft. Rub the fruit through a sieve. When cold stir in the brandy. Whisk the egg whites until stiff and fold into the damson purée with the cream. Spoon into 4 glasses or a bowl.

8ᵗʰ October

EVE'S PUDDING
Serves 4 - 6

450g, 1lb cooking apples, peeled, cored and sliced
50g, 2oz demerara sugar
grated rind and juice of 1 lemon
75g, 3oz butter
75g, 3oz caster sugar
1 egg, beaten
100g, 4oz self-raising flour
a little milk

Grease a round 900ml, 1½pt ovenproof dish. Place the apples in the bottom of the dish. Sprinkle the demerara sugar, lemon rind and juice, and one tablespoon of water over them. Beat the butter with the caster sugar until light and fluffy, then gradually beat in the egg, beating well after each addition. Fold in the flour lightly with a metal spoon, adding a little milk if necessary, to give a soft dropping consistency. Spread over the apples and bake for about 40 minutes in the oven at gas mark 4, 180°C (350°F) until the sponge is cooked through.

9th October

CHOCOLATE RICE PUDDING
Serves 6

900ml, 1½pts milk
100g, 4oz plain chocolate
50g, 2oz short grain pudding rice
75g, 3oz caster sugar
½ tsp vanilla essence
50g, 2oz butter

Heat the milk gently in a saucepan and add the chocolate so that it melts into the milk. Stir in the rice, sugar and vanilla essence. Pour into an ovenproof dish and dot with the butter. Bake in the oven at gas mark 2, 150°C (300°F) for a couple of hours.

10th October

APPLE TURNOVERS
Makes 5

Shortcrust pastry (see page 5)
450g, 1lb cooking apples, peeled, cored and sliced
15g, ½oz butter
grated rind of ½ a lemon
25g, 1oz sultanas
50g, 2oz brown sugar
a little milk and caster sugar

Put the sliced apples, butter, lemon rind, sultanas and sugar in a saucepan and cook for about 5 minutes. Roll out the pastry and cut into 5 large rings, about 12.5cm, 5in in diameter. Put a dollop of apple mixture into each one. Wrap the pastry around the apple and press firmly together. Brush the pastry with milk and dust with caster sugar. Cook in the oven at gas mark 4, 180°C (350°F) for 20 minutes.

11ᵗʰ October
UPSIDE DOWN QUINCE CAKE
Serves 6

Juice of 1 lemon + 2 tbsp sugar
2 medium quinces, peeled, cored and sliced
100g, 4oz butter
175g, 6oz caster sugar
3 eggs
100g, 4oz plain flour
50g, 2oz polenta
50g, 2oz ground almonds
1 tsp vanilla essence

Put 300ml, ½pt of water in a saucepan and add the lemon juice and sugar. Cook the quince slices in this sugar syrup until soft. This should take about 15 minutes. Leave to cool and then arrange them over the base of a greased deep 20cm, 8in cake tin. For the cake, cream together the butter and sugar, then beat in the eggs, and fold in the flour, polenta, almonds and vanilla essence. Spoon on top of the quince slices and bake in the oven at gas mark 4, 180°C (350°F) for 40 minutes. Turn out so that the fruit is on the top. You could use the sugar syrup you poached the quinces in as a sauce. Reduce down by cooking rapidly for a few minutes.

12ᵗʰ October

This is Columbus Day in Argentina and in America as a whole. Celebrations used to occur on 12ᵗʰ October but since the seventies they have taken place on the second Monday in October. Celebrate using dulce de leche, the delicious soft toffee from Argentina.

DULCE DE LECHE CAKE
Serves 6 – 8

Juice of 1 lemon, made up to 120ml, 4 fl oz with water
100g, 4oz butter
3 tbsp golden syrup

225g, 8oz self-raising flour
100g, 4oz light muscovado sugar
1 egg
225g, 8oz dulce de leche
1 tbsp mascarpone

Put the lemon juice and water in a saucepan with the butter and heat gently until the butter has melted. Stir in the golden syrup. Put the flour and sugar in a bowl and beat in the egg followed by the melted butter mixture. Pour into a greased 20cm, 8in round cake tin. Trickle the dulce de leche over the cake and draw a knife over the surface to make streaks. Bake in the oven at gas mark 3, 160°C (325°F) for 30 minutes. Allow to cool. Mix the rest of dulce de leche with the mascarpone and spread over the top of the cake.

13ᵗʰ October

As a variation add 100g, 4oz of blackberries and make this an Apple and Blackberry Pie.

APPLE PIE
Serves 4 - 6

Double quantity shortcrust pastry (see page 5)
450g, 1lb cooking apples, peeled, cored and sliced
100g, 4oz granulated sugar
1 tbsp water
1 tbsp cornflour

Put the apples, sugar and water in a saucepan and simmer gently for about 20 minutes. Blend the cornflour with a little cold water and stir into the fruit. Cook for a couple of minutes until the mixture is thick. Roll out the pastry into two rounds, one slightly bigger than the other. Use the larger half to line the base of a greased 20cm, 8in pie dish. Pour the fruit onto the pastry. Cover with the pastry lid and seal round the edges using a little cold water. Make a little slit in the top of the pie for the steam to escape. Brush with a little milk and a sprinkling of caster sugar. Bake in the oven at gas mark 6, 200°C (400°F) for about 40 minutes.

14ᵗʰ October

STICKY CHOCOLATE AND WALNUT PUDDING
Serves 4 - 6

Fudge Sauce
50g, 2oz butter
75g, 3oz brown sugar
150ml, ¼pt single cream

120ml, 4 fl oz boiling water
100g, 4oz dates, chopped + ½ tsp bicarbonate of soda
75g, 3oz butter
50g, 2oz brown sugar
1 egg
100g, 4oz self-raising flour + 1 tbsp cocoa powder
75g, 3oz walnuts, chopped

Heat the butter and sugar together in a saucepan and stir in the cream. Bring to the boil and boil for a couple of minutes. Use half this sauce to cover the bottom of a greased baking dish. Pour the boiling water over the dates and add the bicarbonate of soda. Leave to stand for a few minutes. Meanwhile for the sponge, cream the butter and sugar together and beat in the egg. Sift the flour and cocoa together and gradually incorporate the flour, walnuts and dates with their liquid into the mixture. Stir together until evenly combined and spoon over the fudge sauce. Cook in the oven at gas mark 4, 180°C (350°F) for about 30 minutes or until the sponge is cooked through. Serve with the rest of the fudge sauce, either poured over the top or served separately.

15ᵗʰ October

MAPLE SYRUP AND APPLE SPONGE
Serves 4 - 6

120ml, 4fl oz maple syrup

450g, 1lb cooking apples, peeled, cored and thinly sliced
3 eggs
75g, 3oz golden caster sugar
75g, 3oz plain flour

Pour the maple syrup into the bottom of a 20cm, 8in pie dish. Cover with slices of apple. Make the sponge by whisking the eggs and sugar together until the mixture is thick enough to leave a trail across the surface. Sift the flour over the mixture and carefully fold in. Spread over the apples and bake in the oven at gas mark 4, 180°C (350°F) for 25 minutes. Turn out so that the apples are on the top.

16ᵗʰ October

CAPE GOOSEBERRY AND PEAR CRUMBLE
Serves 6

1kg, 2lb pears, peeled, cored and sliced
juice of 1 lemon
2 tbsp granulated sugar
100g, 4oz cape gooseberries
2 tbsp dried cranberries

Oaty Crumble
75g, 3oz plain flour
50g, 2oz porridge oats
50g, 2oz ground almonds
75g, 3oz butter
50g, 2oz brown sugar

Put the pears in a saucepan with the lemon, sugar, cape goosberries and cranberries. Heat gently and cook for a few minutes. Transfer to a baking dish. Put the flour and oats in a bowl with the ground almonds. Add the butter and rub with the fingertips until the mixture resembles breadcrumbs. Stir in the brown sugar. Cover the fruit with the crumble mixture and bake in the oven at gas mark 4, 180°C (350°F) for about 30 minutes. Serve hot with cream.

17ᵗʰ October

Somerset, Dorset and Kent all have traditional apple cake recipes. This one is a combination of all three.

SOMERSET APPLE CAKE
Makes about 10 slices

100g, 4oz butter
175g, 6oz dark brown sugar
2 eggs, beaten
225g, 8oz plain wholemeal flour
1 tsp mixed spice
1 tsp ground cinnamon
2 tsp baking powder
450g, 1lb cooking apples, peeled, cored and chopped
3 tbsp milk
1 tbsp black treacle

Cream the butter and sugar together. Add the eggs, alternately with the flour, spices and baking powder. Fold in the apples, milk and black treacle to make a soft dropping consistency. Turn into a greased 20cm, 8in cake tin and bake for an hour in the oven at gas mark 3, 160°C (325°F). Serve warm with Greek yoghurt or crème fraîche.

18ᵗʰ October

APPLE AND CARDAMOM WITH HAZELNUT CRUMBLE
Serves 4 - 6

675g, 1½lb cooking apples, peeled, cored and sliced
75g, 3oz granulated sugar
6 – 8 cardamom pods

Crumble
150g, 5oz plain flour
75g, 3oz soft brown sugar

100g, 4oz butter
50g, 2oz hazelnuts, chopped

Layer the apples in a baking dish and sprinkle with the granulated sugar. Extract the seeds from the cardamom pods and lightly crush them with a pestle and mortar. Add to the apples. Mix the flour with the brown sugar and rub in the butter. Stir in the hazelnuts and sprinkle over the apple mixture. Cook at gas mark 4, 180°C (350°F) for 30 minutes. Serve hot with cream.

19ᵗʰ October

APPLE AND LEMON TARTLETS
Makes 4 tartlets

Shortcrust pastry (see page 5)
450g, 1lb cooking apples, peeled, cored and thinly sliced
3 eggs
75g, 3oz caster sugar
150ml, ¼pt single cream
grated rind and juice of 1 lemon

Roll out the pastry and divide into four circles to fit into a greased tartlet tin. Bake blind in the oven at gas mark 4, 180°C (350°F) for 15 minutes. Beat the eggs, cream and sugar together. Add the grated lemon rind and juice and whisk until smooth. Arrange the apple slices in the tartlets and cover with the egg and lemon mixture. Return to the oven and bake for about 25 minutes. Turn out and serve warm.

20th October

Have a break from all those fruity puddings.

DOUBLE CHOCOLATE TERRINE
Serves 6

1 whisked chocolate sponge, (see page 6) baked in a square tin

Plain chocolate layer
100g, 4oz plain chocolate
1 tbsp brandy
1 egg
200ml, 7fl oz double cream, whipped

White chocolate layer
75g, 3oz white chocolate
1 egg
150ml, ¼pt double cream, whipped

Cut the sponge in half and put one half in the bottom of a loaf tin lined with cling film. Make the plain chocolate layer by melting the chocolate with the brandy, and stirring until smooth. Whisk the egg until thick and fold into the chocolate. Fold in the whipped cream and spoon over the cake base. Place in the freezer for 15 minutes to firm up. Make the white chocolate layer in the same way. Melt the white chocolate, stir into the whisked egg and fold in the cream. Pour on top of the plain chocolate layer and put back in the freezer for another 15 minutes. Cover with the remaining chocolate sponge and chill until ready to serve. Turn out onto a serving plate and remove the cling film. Slice thinly to serve.

21st October

This is official Apple Day and *Common Ground* organise a list of Apple Day Events across the country. This is a delicious pudding. It's lovely and gooey and needs to be served with cream or crème fraîche.

APPLE FUDGE PUDDING
Serves 4 - 6

Sponge
150g, 5oz plain flour
1 tsp baking powder
2 tbsp caster sugar
50g, 2oz butter
1 large egg
½ tsp vanilla essence
90ml, 3fl oz milk

Topping
450g, 1lb cooking apples, peeled and cored
50g, 2oz butter
175g, 6oz dark brown or muscovado sugar
1 tsp ground cinnamon

To make the sponge, mix together the flour, baking powder and sugar. Add the butter using your fingertips as though you were making pastry until the mixture is like breadcrumbs. Whisk the egg and vanilla essence together and add the milk. Stir into the flour and butter mixture and transfer the batter to a buttered rectangular ovenproof dish measuring about 25 x 20cm, 10 by 8in. Slice the apples and spread over the batter. Melt together the butter, sugar and cinnamon and spread over the apple. Bake in the oven at gas mark 4, 180°C (350°F) for 30 minutes. Serve with cream or crème fraîche.

22nd October

CHOCOLATE, PEAR AND RASPBERRY
UPSIDE DOWN PUDDING
Serves 6 – 8

50g, 2oz butter
50g, 2oz caster sugar
3 pears, peeled and sliced
100g, 4oz raspberries

Sponge
150g, 5oz self-raising flour
50g, 2oz cocoa powder
100g, 4oz butter
100g, 4oz caster sugar
2 eggs
2 tbsp milk

Chocolate sauce
100g, 4oz plain chocolate
300ml, ½pt water
50g, 2oz butter

To make the topping, cream the butter and sugar together and spread over the base of a 20cm, 8in cake tin. Arrange the pear slices and raspberries over the sugar. To make the sponge, sift the flour and cocoa together. Cream the butter and sugar and gradually stir in the eggs with the milk and a little of the flour. Beat in the rest of the flour. Spoon over the fruit and bake in the oven at gas mark 4, 180°C (350°F) for 40 minutes. Invert the pudding onto a plate and serve with chocolate sauce if liked. For the sauce melt the chocolate in the water, stirring until smooth. Remove from the heat and add the butter. Stir until the butter has melted and the sauce is smooth.

23rd October

CARAMEL APPLE AND DATE MUFFIN CAKE
Serves 6 – 8

150g, 5oz granulated sugar
2 tbsp water
4 red eating apples, cored and sliced, with skin left on
50g, 2oz dates, chopped
225g, 8oz self-raising flour
100g, 4oz caster sugar
2 eggs
200ml, 7fl oz buttermilk
50g, 2oz butter, melted

Make a caramel syrup by gently heating the sugar and water in a frying pan until the sugar has dissolved. Then cook without stirring until it turns a golden caramel. Add the sliced apples and the dates and cook for a minute or so. Then transfer to a greased 20cm, 8in cake tin. To make the muffin mixture put the flour and sugar in a bowl. Beat the eggs in a separate bowl with the buttermilk and melted butter. Stir into the flour mixture to make a batter. Pour over the apple and dates. Cook in the oven at gas mark 4, 180°C (350°F) for 25 minutes. Leave to cool slightly before turning out. Serve with cream or vanilla ice cream.

24th October

CHESTNUT CHARLOTTE
Serves 6

18 sponge fingers
450g, 1lb tin of unsweetened chestnut purée
50g, 2oz caster sugar
50g, 2oz butter
100g, 4oz melted chocolate
1 tbsp espresso coffee liquid
1 tsp vanilla essence
300ml, ½pt double cream, whipped

Place the sponge fingers around the base and sides of a charlotte mould. Mix together the chestnut purée, sugar, butter, melted chocolate, coffee, vanilla and brandy. Fold in the double cream. Pour into the mould and chill for a few hours before turning out.

25th October

CARROT AND APPLE TART
Serves 4 – 6

175g, 6oz shortcrust pastry
25g, 1oz brown breadcrumbs
50g, 2oz carrot, peeled and grated
2 eating apples, cored, peeled and grated
50g, 2oz butter, melted
150ml, ¼pt single cream
1 tbsp lemon juice
50g, 2oz caster sugar
1 whole egg and 1 egg yolk

Line a 17.5cm, 7in greased flan tin with the pastry. Put the breadcrumbs, carrot and apple in a mixing bowl and beat in the butter, cream, lemon juice, sugar, whole egg and egg yolk. When all is thoroughly combined pour onto the pastry base and bake in the oven on a baking tray (this helps prevent the pastry becoming soggy) at gas mark 4, 180°C (350°F) for 25 minutes.

26ᵗʰ October

Punky Night is the last Thursday in October and is a Somerset tradition. In the Middle Ages all the men of Hinton St George went off to a fair. When they failed to return that evening the women went looking for them by the light of Punkies (pumpkins hollowed out and with a candle placed inside). Traditionally children in the South of England would make their pumpkins into Jack O'Lanterns and would go out singing traditional punky songs and competing for the best lanterns. This tradition still takes place in Hinton St George.

PUMPKIN CAKE
Serves 6 - 8

175g, 6oz wholemeal flour + 2 tsp baking powder
1 tsp ground cinnamon
100g, 4oz grated pumpkin or squash
100g, 4oz butter
100g, 4oz dark brown sugar
grated rind of 1 lemon
2 eggs + 2 tbsp milk

Filling
50g, 2oz butter
100g, 4oz icing sugar
2 tsp lemon juice
grated rind of ½ a lemon

Put all the ingredients in a food processor and whizz until smooth or sift together the flour, baking powder and cinnamon. Add the grated pumpkin. Cream the butter and brown sugar together. Beat the eggs and add to the butter and sugar mixture, adding a little flour if the mixture begins to curdle. Gradually add all the flour and pumpkin along with the grated lemon rind and mix in the milk. Divide between 2 greased 15cm, 6in round cake tins and bake in the oven at gas mark 4, 180°C (350°F) for 25 minutes. Meanwhile make the filling by creaming together the butter and icing sugar and beating in the lemon juice and rind. Use this filling to sandwich the cakes together. Dust with icing sugar and serve.

27ᵗʰ October

LEMON RICE PUDDING
Serves 4 - 6

50g, 2oz pudding rice
50g, 2oz caster sugar
large piece of pared lemon rind
600ml, 1pt milk
2 egg yolks
1 tsp lemon juice

Put the rice into an ovenproof dish along with the caster sugar and piece of lemon rind. Pour over the milk. Cook for 2 hours in the oven at gas mark 2, 150°C (300°F) until creamy. Add a little more milk if the pudding becomes too dry. Beat the egg yolks with the lemon juice. Add a little of the hot milk from the rice, then stir the mixture into the creamed rice. Return to the oven for a further 20 minutes. Remove the lemon rind and serve with cream.

With the left over egg whites make **Meringue Biscuits**. Whisk the 2 egg whites until stiff, fold in 100g, 4oz of caster sugar and 100g, 4oz ground almonds. Put spoonfuls on greased baking sheets and bake for 10 minutes in the oven at gas mark 5, 190°C (375°F). Dip to half-cover in some melted chocolate, leave to harden and serve with the rice pudding.

28ᵗʰ October

APPLE FLAPJACK PUDDING
Serves 4 - 6

100g, 4oz butter, melted
150g, 5oz porridge oats
75g, 3oz soft brown sugar
5 cooking apples, peeled, cored and thinly sliced + a little water

Combine the butter, oats and sugar and beat until blended together. In a serving dish layer the oat mixture alternately with a layer of apples. Finish with a layer of the flapjack mixture. Bake in the oven at gas mark 4, 180°C (350°F) for 40 minutes. Serve with cream.

29ᵗʰ October

QUINCE AND GINGER CRUMBLE
Serves 6

450g, 1lb quinces, peeled, cored and chopped
450g, 1lb cooking apples, peeled, cored and sliced + 2 tbsp water
100g, 4oz granulated sugar

For the crumble
175g, 6oz plain flour
2 tsp ground ginger
75g, 3oz butter
50g, 2oz brown sugar

Cook the apples and quinces with the water and granulated sugar for 5 – 10 minutes to soften them. Transfer to a baking dish. To make the crumble combine all the ingredients in a food processor and process until the mixture resembles breadcrumbs. Spread evenly over the fruit and bake in the oven at gas mark 4, 180°C (350°F) for about 30 minutes.

30ᵗʰ October

SEMI FREDDO BANANA CREAM
Serves 4

4 ripe bananas
300ml, ½pt double cream
50g, 2oz ground almonds
50g, 2oz light brown sugar
2 tbsp brandy

Mash the bananas. Whisk the cream and mix into the bananas with the ground almonds, sugar and brandy. Spoon into a dish and freeze for a couple of hours before serving.

31ˢᵗ October

For Halloween it's got to be something warming and related to pumpkins.

MINI PUMPKIN AND GINGER PUDDINGS
Serves 6

60g, 2½oz butter
50g, 2oz brown sugar
3 eggs
150g, 5oz plain flour
1 tsp bicarbonate of soda
175g, 6oz pumpkin purée
½ tsp ground ginger
¼ tsp ground nutmeg

Maple Syrup Sauce
75g, 3oz butter
6 tbsp maple syrup
150ml, ¼pt whipping cream

Cream together the butter and sugar. Beat in the eggs one at a time and then stir in the flour sifted with the bicarbonate of soda, pumpkin purée, ginger and nutmeg. Divide between 6 buttered mini pudding basins and put into a deep baking dish. Pour enough water into the dish to come halfway up the sides of the moulds. Bake for 20 minutes at gas mark 4, 180°C (350°F) or until cooked through. To make the sauce melt the butter and stir in the syrup and the cream. Bring to the boil and boil for 5 minutes by which time it should have become the colour of butterscotch. Turn out the puddings and serve with the maple syrup sauce and with vanilla ice cream if feeling really indulgent.

1ˢᵗ November

CARAMELISED APPLE SPONGE
Serves 4 – 6

50g, 2oz butter
3 tbsp demerara sugar
2 tbsp cider vinegar
450g, 1lb eating apples, peeled, cored and chopped

Sponge
100g, 4oz butter
100g, 4oz caster sugar
2 eggs
100g, 4oz self-raising flour

First put the butter and sugar in a saucepan and heat gently. When the butter has melted, turn up the heat and, stirring with a wooden spoon, let the mixture bubble and darken. Add the vinegar (be careful, the mixture will splutter) and drop in the sliced apples. Cook for about 15 minutes, turning the apples every so often. Try not to allow them to break up. Transfer to a dish and leave to cool. For the sponge, combine all four ingredients in a food processor or cream the butter and sugar together and add the eggs gradually with the flour. Spread half the sponge mixture over the base of a greased pie dish, pour the apples over this and cover with the rest of the sponge mixture. Bake in the oven at gas mark 4, 180°C (350°F) for 30 minutes. Stick a skewer in to make sure the sponge is cooked in the middle.

2ⁿᵈ November

This is All Souls Day when the dead are remembered. On this day the poor and their children would walk from village to village begging for soul cakes. In return the poor would offer prayers for the dead. It was believed the dead remained in limbo for a time after death and that prayer could help a soul's passage to heaven. The beggars would sing a song :

'Soul! Soul! For a Soul Cake!
I pray you good missis, a Soul Cake,
An apple, a pear, a plum or cherry,
Or any good thing to make us all merry.
One for Peter and two for Paul, three for Him that made us all'.

SOUL CAKES
Makes 24

175g, 6oz butter
175g, 6oz caster sugar
3 egg yolks
450g, 1lb plain flour
1 tsp mixed spice
75g, 3oz currants

Cream the butter and sugar together and then beat in the egg yolks. Sift the flour and mixed spice and fold into the egg mixture with the currants, adding a little milk to make a soft dough. Divide into flat cakes, marking each with a cross. Place on greased baking sheet and bake in the oven at gas mark 4, 180°C (350°F) for 20 minutes.

Make meringues with the left over egg whites.

3rd November

LOG FIRE GINGERBREAD PUDDING
Serves 8

100g, 4oz brown sugar
50g, 2oz butter
3 Granny Smiths or other crisp eating apples, peeled,
cored and sliced

Gingerbread
100g, 4oz plain flour
½ tsp bicarbonate of soda
½ tsp ground nutmeg
1 tsp ground ginger
2 tsp ground cinnamon
pinch of ground cloves
1 egg
100g, 4oz soft brown sugar
3 tbsp black treacle
150ml, ¼pt milk
50g, 2oz melted butter

To make the base, melt the butter and sugar together and spread it over the bottom of an ovenproof dish. Arrange the sliced apples on top of the brown sugar mixture. Sift the flour with the bicarbonate of soda and the spices, then mix in the egg, sugar, treacle, milk and melted butter and beat it until the mixture is smooth. Pour it over the apples and bake in the oven at gas mark 4, 180°C (350°F) for about 45 minutes. Serve with whipped cream.

4ᵗʰ November

This is Mischief Night. The roots for this tradition can be traced to Yorkshire and Lancashire. Traditional mischiefs were: knocking on doors and windows, smearing doorknobs with treacle, draping rolls of loo paper over trees and buildings and throwing eggs at people's homes and cars. Instead why not use your treacle and eggs to make a treacle pudding! This is a simple steamed pudding but great for a family supper.

TREACLE PUDDING
Serves 4 – 6

2 tbsp golden syrup
100g, 4oz self-raising flour
100g, 4oz caster sugar
2 eggs
100g, 4oz butter
golden syrup for serving

Spread the golden syrup over the bottom and sides of a 1.2 litre, 2 pint pudding basin. Put the flour, sugar, eggs and butter into a food processor and process until well mixed. Put the golden syrup into the bottom of a pudding basin and spread it around the sides. Spoon the sponge mixture into the basin and cover loosely with greaseproof papr and secure with a rubber band. Put the pudding basin in a steamer and cook for about an hour. Turn out onto a serving dish and serve with golden syrup warmed for easy pouring and cream if liked.

5ᵗʰ November

This is Guy Fawkes Night. Traditionally Parkin is made for Bonfire Night but it is best made a week before you intend to eat it.

PARKIN
Makes 12 – 16 pieces

225g, 8oz self-raising flour
225g, 8oz medium oatmeal
1 tsp ground ginger
½ tsp ground cinnamon
¼ tsp ground nutmeg
75g, 3oz brown sugar
100g, 4oz butter
100g, 4oz black treacle
100g, 4oz golden syrup
90ml, 3 fl oz milk

Mix together the flour, oatmeal, spices and sugar. Melt the butter and the treacle and syrup together and add to the dry ingredients. Stir in the milk. Cook in a greased baking tin for 1 hour at gas mark 2, 150°C (300°F). Cool and cut into squares.

6ᵗʰ November

APPLE AND GINGERBREAD TRIFLE
Serves 6 - 8

225g, 8oz gingerbread (see page 209)
675g, 1½lb cooking apples, peeled, cored and sliced
2 tbsp golden syrup
1 tbsp black treacle
1 tbsp brown sugar
150ml, ¼pt double cream
150ml, ¼pt Greek yoghurt

Slice the gingerbread and place in the bottom of a glass serving bowl. Put the apples in a saucepan with the syrup, treacle and brown sugar. Bring to the boil and then simmer until the apples are soft and you have a dark purée. Spoon over the gingerbread. Whip together the double cream and yoghurt and spread over the top of the apple. Chill before serving.

7ᵗʰ November

LEMON AND HAZELNUT ROULADE WITH CHOCOLATE CREAM
Serves 8

For the roulade
5 eggs, separated
150g, 5oz caster sugar
grated rind and juice of 1 lemon
50g, 2oz ground hazelnuts

For the filling
300ml, ½pt double cream
75g, 3oz dark chocolate, grated
50g, 2oz white chocolate, grated
sprinkling of icing sugar

Line a Swiss roll tin with greaseproof paper. To make the roulade, whisk the egg yolks in a bowl, gradually adding the caster sugar and whisking until the mixture is pale and thick. Whisk in the lemon juice and fold in the ground hazelnuts and grated lemon rind. Whisk the egg whites until stiff and fold them into the lemon mixture. Pour into the Swiss roll tin. Bake in the oven at gas mark 4, 180°C (350°F) for about 20 minutes. Take out the roulade and cover with a damp tea towel. Leave for a few hours. To make the filling, whip the cream until thick but not too stiff. Fold in the grated chocolate. Place a piece of greaseproof paper on your work surface and cover with icing sugar. Tip the roulade out onto the icing sugar. Carefully peel off the lining paper. Spread the cream over the roulade and roll up.

8ᵗʰ November

MAPLE SYRUP NUTTY CAKE
Serves 6

50g, 2oz walnuts, halved
50g, 2oz pecans, halved

175g, 6oz butter
175g, 6oz caster sugar
3 eggs
175g, 6oz self-raising flour
2 tsp mixed spice
5 tbsp maple syrup

Toast the nuts under the grill until golden. Arrange in the base of a greased 20cm, 8in cake tin. Cream the butter and sugar and gradually beat in the eggs. Fold in the flour, mixed spice and 2 tablespoons of maple syrup. Spoon this mixture over the nuts and bake for 1 hour in the oven at gas mark 5, 190°C (375°F). Leave to cool in the tin for a few minutes, then turn out onto a plate so that the nuts are uppermost. Pour the remaining maple syrup over the cake and serve. Serve with cream if liked.

9th November

Save two egg whites for the Prune Soufflé tomorrow.

CHOCOLATE AND CHESTNUT ICE CREAM
Serves 6 – 8

3 egg yolks
225g, 8oz caster sugar
300ml, ½pt single cream
225g, 8oz can of unsweetened chestnut purée
100g, 4oz plain chocolate
3 tbsp brandy
300ml, ½pt double cream, beaten

Whisk the egg yolks with the sugar until thick. Warm the single cream until just below boiling point. Add a little to the chestnut purée to form a smooth paste. Add the chocolate to the remaining cream and leave until melted. Stir until smooth and then pour over the yolks and stir to combine. Add the chestnut purée. Leave to cool and then stir in the brandy and fold in the cream. Transfer to a freezer container and freeze until firm.

10ᵗʰ November

PRUNE SOUFFLÉ
Serves 3 - 4

2 egg whites (from yesterday)
225g, 8oz dried prunes, puréed with a little water
50g, 2oz caster sugar

Beat the egg whites until stiff and fold in the sugar and prune purée. Transfer to a small baking dish and bake in the oven at gas mark 2, 150°C (300°F) for 20 minutes. Serve with Greek yoghurt or cream.

11ᵗʰ November

CARAMEL STEAMED PUDDING
Serves 4 - 6

50g, 2oz granulated sugar
1 tbsp water
150ml, ¼pt milk
100g, 4oz butter
100g, 4oz caster sugar
2 eggs, separated
175g, 6oz plain flour
½ tsp baking powder

Dissolve the sugar over a gentle heat in the tablespoon of water and boil until it turns a caramel colour. Warm the milk and add to the caramel. Stir until the caramel dissolves into the milk. Leave to cool. Cream the butter and caster sugar and add the egg yolks. Stir in the flour sifted with the baking powder alternately with the caramel milk. Whisk the egg whites and fold them in. Pour into a greased pudding basin, cover and steam for 1 hour. Turn out and serve with butterscotch sauce (see page 28 or 121) or chocolate sauce (see page 7 or 12) and or cream.

12ᵗʰ November

APPLE AND DATE BROWN BETTY
Serves 4

6 tbsp breadcrumbs
675g, 1½lb cooking apples, cored, peeled and sliced
75g, 3oz pitted dates, chopped
25g, 1oz butter, melted
1 tbsp lemon juice
3 tbsp maple syrup
1 tbsp brown sugar

Grease a baking dish and sprinkle some breadcrumbs on the base. Make layers of sliced apples, dates and breadcrumbs. Mix together the melted butter, lemon juice and maple syrup and pour over the apple. Sprinkle with the tablespoon of brown sugar. Bake in the oven at gas mark 4, 180°C (350°F) for about 45 minutes until the apple is soft. This is delicious with a dollop of crème fraîche.

13ᵗʰ November

Save the egg whites for tomorrow's Chocolate Meringue Roulade.

HAZELNUT ICE CREAM
Serves 6 - 8

175g, 6oz granulated sugar
120ml, 4 fl oz water
5 egg yolks
300ml, ½pt double cream, whipped
75g, 3oz hazelnuts, toasted and ground

Combine the sugar and water in a saucepan and heat gently until the sugar dissolves. Boil for 5 minutes. Beat the egg yolks until thick and continue to whisk as you pour in the sugar syrup. Whisk until cooled and then fold in the double cream and the hazelnuts. Pour into a freezer container and freeze.

14th November

CHOCOLATE MERINGUE ROULADE
Serves 6

4 egg whites (from yesterday)
225g, 8oz caster sugar
1 tsp cornflour
1 tsp white wine vinegar
1 tsp vanilla essence
300ml, ½pt double cream
100g, 4oz plain chocolate, grated
icing sugar for sprinkling

Whisk the egg whites until stiff. Then whisk in the caster sugar a tablespoon at a time. Blend together the cornflour, vinegar and vanilla essence and fold into the meringue mixture. Line a Swiss roll tin with greaseproof paper and gently spread out the meringue mixture in the tin. Bake in the oven at gas mark 2, 150°C (300°F) for 40 minutes by which time the meringue should be crisp on the outside. Remove from the oven and leave to cool before turning out onto a piece of greaseproof paper. Peel off the lining paper. Whip the cream and mix in grated chocolate. Spread this mixture over the roulade. Roll up the roulade from one of the short ends using the paper to help you. Don't worry if the roulade cracks – this is normal. Sprinkle with icing sugar if liked.

15th November
APPLE AND GRAPE PIE
Serves 6 – 8

Double quantity shortcrust pastry (see page 5)
100g, 4oz granulated sugar
½ tsp ground cinnamon
¼ tsp ground nutmeg
2 large cooking apples, peeled, cored and sliced
350g, 12oz seedless green grapes

1 tbsp cornflour mixed with 2 tbsp water
25g, 1oz butter
1 egg, beaten

Roll out two circles of pastry, one slightly larger than the other and use to line a greased 20cm, 8in pie dish. Mix together the sugar, cinnamon and nutmeg and stir in the apple slices, grapes and cornflour paste. Spoon into the pie dish and top with the remaining pastry circle. Press the edges to seal together and cut slits in the pastry top to allow steam to escape. Brush with beaten egg. Bake in the oven at gas mark 4, 180°C (350°F) for 40 minutes or until golden brown.

16ᵗʰ November

FUDGE AND CHOCOLATE CREAM TART
Serves 6

175g, 6oz digestive biscuits, crushed
75g, 3oz butter, melted
60ml, 2fl oz water
175g, 6oz granulated sugar
1 tbsp golden syrup
50g, 2oz butter
60ml, 2fl oz double cream

Topping
200ml, 7fl oz double cream
100g, 4oz plain chocolate

Mix the biscuit crumbs into the melted butter and use to line a greased 20cm, 8in flan tin. Heat the water, sugar and golden syrup in a small saucepan and when the sugar has dissolved bring to the boil and cook until a golden brown colour. Whisk in the butter and stir in the cream. Pour into the tart shell and leave to cool – the mixture will thicken as it cools. Heat the cream and stir in the chocolate. Stir together until the chocolate has melted and pour over the fudgy filling. Leave to set.

17ᵗʰ November

These are floating islands of poached meringues topped with caramel and surrounded by custard.

OEUFS A LA NEIGE
Serves 4 – 6

600ml, 1pt milk
1 tsp vanilla essence
5 eggs, separated
150g, 5oz caster sugar
50g, 2oz icing sugar
2 tbsp water

To make the custard, heat the milk in a saucepan with the vanilla essence. Mix the egg yolks with 75g, 3oz of sugar in a bowl and stir into the milk. Bring slowly to just below boiling point and stir until the mixture thickens. Allow to cool. Heat a saucepan of water. Whisk the egg whites until stiff and whisk in the icing sugar. Using a large spoon carefully lower a spoonful of egg white mixture into the water and cook for about 15 seconds on each side. Place on a wire rack. Continue cooking spoonfuls of meringue and drying them on a wire rack. When ready to serve place them on top of the custard in a serving dish. Dissolve the remaining 50g, 2oz of sugar in the two tablespoons of water. Boil until caramel coloured. Pour over the egg shapes and serve immediately.

18ᵗʰ November

MINI AUTUMN PUDDINGS
Serves 6

10 slices of wholemeal bread, crusts removed
3 large cooking apples, peeled and sliced
3 pears, peeled and diced
225g, 8oz autumn raspberries + 100g, 4oz blackcurrants
175g, 6oz granulated sugar

Line 6 mini pudding basins with the bread. Put the apples and pears in a saucepan with the sugar and 300ml, ½pt water, bring to the boil and then simmer for 10 minutes. Add the raspberries and blackcurrants and cook for a further 5 minutes. Leave to cool and pour fruit and some of the syrup into each pudding basin. Top with a circle of bread and leave to chill.

19ᵗʰ November

CARAMEL CHEESECAKE
Serves 6

For the base
50g, 2oz butter
25g, 1oz porridge oats
75g, 3oz plain flour
75g, 3oz caster sugar

For the filling
225g, 8oz cream cheese
2 eggs, separated
100g, 4oz brown sugar
4 tbsp dulce de leche
1 tbsp cornflour
150ml, ¼pt double cream

Topping
100g, 4oz granulated sugar + 3 tbsp water

For the base melt the butter and stir in the oats, flour and sugar. Press onto the base of a greased 20cm, 8in loose-bottomed round cake tin. Bake in the oven at gas mark 3, 160°C (325°F) for 10 minutes. Beat the cream cheese and beat in the egg yolks and brown sugar. Fold in the dulce de leche, cornflour and double cream. Whisk the egg whites and fold into the cheesecake mixture. Return to the oven for 1 hour. For the topping, dissolve the sugar in the water and boil until golden brown. Pour evenly over the top of the cheesecake. Allow to cool and turn out.

20ᵗʰ November

SPONGE AND CHOCOLATE
UPSIDE DOWN PUDDING
Serves 6 – 8

Fudge topping
40g, 1½oz butter
40g, 1½oz brown sugar
40g, 1½oz golden syrup
15g, ½oz cocoa powder
2 tbsp single cream

100g, 4oz caster sugar
100g, 4oz butter
100g, 4oz self-raising flour
1 tsp baking powder
2 eggs

Place all the ingredients for the fudgy chocolate sauce in a small saucepan and heat gently, then boil for a minute. Pour into a greased 20cm, 8in cake tin and leave to cool. Beat together all the ingredients for the sponge and spoon on top of the chocolate. Bake in the oven at gas mark 3, 160°C (325°F) for 40 minutes. Leave in the tin for a few minutes before turning out so that the chocolate sauce is on top. Serve hot with cream or ice cream.

21ˢᵗ November

Save the egg yolks and make custard for tomorrow's Guards Pudding.

MONT BLANC
Serves 4

3 egg whites
175g, 6oz caster sugar
450g, 1lb chestnut purée, unsweetened

150g, 5oz icing sugar
1 tsp vanilla essence
1 tbsp brandy
150ml, ¼pt double cream, whipped

First make four meringue nests by whisking the egg whites until very stiff, then whisk in half the caster sugar. Fold in the rest of the sugar and place large spoonfuls on greased baking sheets, indenting them in the middle so that they look like nests. Bake in the oven at gas mark 1, 140°C (275°F) for an hour. Meanwhile mix or process together the chestnut purée, icing sugar, vanilla essence and brandy. Spoon some of this chestnut mixture into each meringue nest and top with a spoonful of cream.

22nd November

GUARDS PUDDING
Serves 4 - 6

100g, 4oz butter
100g, 4oz caster sugar
75g, 3oz self-raising flour
75g, 3oz fresh white breadcrumbs
3 eggs
3 tbsp raspberry jam

Cream the butter and sugar together. Beat in the eggs alternately with the flour and breadcrumbs. Fold in the jam. Spoon into a greased pudding basin, cover with greaseproof paper and steam for an hour. Turn out and serve with custard if liked, using yesterday's egg yolks (see page 5).

23rd November

LEMON SYRUP TART
Serves 6 – 8

Shortcrust pastry (see page 5)
175g, 6oz golden syrup
50g, 2oz butter
300ml, ½pt crème fraîche
2 eggs, beaten
grated rind and juice of 1 large lemon
icing sugar for dusting

Roll out the pastry and line a greased 23cm, 9in flan dish. Prick and bake blind in the oven at gas mark 5, 190°C (375°F) for about 15 minutes. Meanwhile warm the golden syrup in a saucepan with the butter. Remove from the heat and whisk in the crème fraîche , beaten eggs, and the grated lemon rind and juice. Pour onto the pastry base and bake in the oven at gas mark 4, 180°C (350°F) for 30 minutes or until the surface is set. The filling may be a little wobbly in the middle but will firm up on cooling. Dust with icing sugar before serving.

24th November

It's nearly Thanksgiving in America. A thin crisp meringue forms on top of this pecan pie which is a traditional pie from Texas.

TEXAS OSGOOD PECAN PIE
Serves 6 - 8

Shortcrust pastry (see page 5)
175g, 6oz caster sugar
100g, 4oz butter
¼ tsp ground cinnamon + pinch of cloves
1 tsp vanilla essence
1 tsp white wine vinegar
4 eggs, separated
150g, 5oz chopped pecans
150g, 5oz chopped dates

Roll out the pastry and use to line a greased 23cm, 9in flan tin. Beat together the sugar and butter. Add the cinnamon, pinch of cloves, vanilla essence, vinegar and egg yolks. Stir in the pecans and dates. Beat the egg whites until stiff. Fold them carefully into the mixture. Spoon into the pastry and level the surface. Bake in the oven at gas mark 3, 160°C (325°F) for 35 minutes.

25th November

This is St Catherine's day. St Catherine was Patron Saint of lace makers. Somehow St Catherine was connected with the banished Catherine of Aragon who lived during some of her life at Ampthill Castle in Bedfordshire. Catherine of Aragon apparently introduced lace-making into Bedfordshire. 'Wiggs' or Cattern cakes were eaten traditionally when the lace makers celebrated on 25th November. In Somerset Cattern cakes or pie were shaped like a Catherine Wheel with a filling of mincemeat. Catherine Wheels were spun and sparkled for the saint and girls would jump over lighted candles. St Catherine's Day is said to usher in the winter.

CATTERN PIE
Serves 4 - 6

Shortcrust pastry (see page 5)
300ml, ½pt apple purée
225g, 8oz mincemeat

Line a greased 20cm, 8in flan tin with the pastry, save any bits left over, roll them out and cut into strips. Fill the dish with a layer of mincemeat and then a layer of apple. Make spokes from your strips of pastry and lay them across to form a wheel. Bake in the oven at gas mark 4, 180°C (350°F) until the pastry is cooked, which should be about 20 minutes.

Making your Christmas Pudding
Around this time it is Stir-up Sunday - the last Sunday before Advent which is traditionally the time to make the Christmas pudding. Turn to Christmas Day on page 245 for the recipe.

26ᵗʰ November

Try this cheesecake – it's unbaked so quick to prepare.

EASY CHOCOLATE CHEESECAKE
Serves 6

175g, 6oz digestive biscuits, crushed
50g, 2oz butter
50g, 2oz brown sugar
225g, 8oz cream cheese
2 eggs, separated
100g, 4oz caster sugar
100g, 4oz plain chocolate, melted
300ml, ½pt double cream

Melt the butter and mix in the biscuit crumbs and brown sugar. Press onto the base of a greased 20cm, 8in flan tin and bake in the oven for 10 minutes at gas mark 3, 160°C (325°F). Remove and cool. Beat the cream cheese and beat in the egg yolks and caster sugar. Fold in the chocolate and double cream. Whisk the egg whites until stiff and fold into the cheesecake mixture. Spoon onto the biscuit base. Chill before serving.

27ᵗʰ November

Thanksgiving Day is a national holiday in America and is celebrated on the fourth Thursday in November, so why not have a go at a couple of American puddings? Pumpkin Pie is the traditional American Thanksgiving Pie and there are many different versions. My version, despite the spices, proved popular with the children.

PUMPKIN PIE
Serves 6 - 8

Shortcrust pastry (see page 5)
175g, 6oz pumpkin purée

75g, 3oz granulated sugar
75g, 3oz molasses
1 small tin of evaporated milk
2 eggs
½ tsp each of ground cinnamon & ground ginger
pinch of ground nutmeg

Roll out the pastry and use to line a greased 20cm, 8in flan dish. Prick and bake blind for 10 minutes in the oven at gas mark 4, 180°C (350°F). Mix together the purée, sugar, molasses, evaporated milk, eggs and spices. Pour into the pastry case and return to the oven for 20 minutes. Serve warm.

28th November

SHOO FLY PIE
Serves 8

Shortcrust pastry (see page 5)
150ml, ¼pt boiling water
4 tbsp golden syrup
4 tbsp molasses
1 tsp baking powder
1 egg, beaten

Crumble topping

75g, 3oz butter
175g, 6oz plain flour
½ tsp ground cinnamon
75g, 3oz light brown sugar

Make the pastry and use to line a greased 23cm, 9in flan dish. Prick and bake blind in the oven at gas mark 4, 180°C (350°F) for 10 minutes. For the filling stir the water and the golden syrup into the molasses. Beat the baking powder into the egg and beat into the molasses mixture. Pour over the pastry base. Make the crumble topping by rubbing the butter into the flour and cinnamon with your fingertips and then stirring in the sugar. Sprinkle over the top. Return to the oven on a hot baking sheet at for 35 minutes.

29th November

Louisa May Alcott, author of *Little Women*, was born on November 29th 1832. Apple Slump was apparently Alcott's favourite pudding and she even nicknamed her house in Massachusetts, 'Apple Slump'. The topping is similar to the mixture for a cobbler.

APPLE SLUMP
Serves 6

1kg, 2lb cooking apples, peeled, cored and sliced
100g, 4oz granulated sugar
1 tsp ground cinnamon
a little water

For the topping
75g, 3oz butter
225g, 8oz self-raising flour
50g, 2oz caster sugar
150ml, ¼pt milk

Put the sliced apples, sugar, cinnamon and a sprinkling of water in a baking dish and cook in the oven for 15 minutes to soften. To make the topping rub the butter into the flour, stir in the sugar and then mix to a dough with the milk. Drop spoonfuls of the dough over the apples. Cook in the oven at gas mark 4, 180°C (350°F) for 30 minutes. Serve hot with cream.

30ᵗʰ November

St Andrew is the Patron Saint of Scotland, and St Andrew's Day is celebrated by Scots around the world on this day. Here is a refreshing dessert which uses marmalade, a popular ingredient in Scottish cooking since its invention in Dundee in 1797.

CALEDONIAN CREAM
Serves 4

100g, 4oz cream cheese
120ml, 4 fl oz double cream
1 tbsp orange marmalade
2 tbsp brandy
2 tsp lemon juice
75g, 3oz caster sugar
4 oranges, segmented with pith removed

Blend all the ingredients except the oranges in a liquidiser till smooth. Place the oranges in four long-stemmed glasses Divide the topping between the glasses. Serve chilled.

1ˢᵗ December

This is National Day in Romania. Romanians celebrate the unification of Romania and Transylvania which happened on 1ˢᵗ December 1918. This cheese soufflé would be great with raspberry or blackcurrant sauce.

ROMANIAN CHEESE SOUFFLÉ
Serves 4

25g, 1oz butter
40g, 1½oz plain flour
25g, 1oz cream cheese
90ml, 3fl oz soured cream
3 eggs, beaten
6 tbsp milk
1 tbsp icing sugar for dusting

Spread the butter over the base of a 20cm, 8in square ovenproof dish and dust with a little of the flour. Beat the cheese with the soured cream. Beat the eggs into the mixture. Add the milk and rest of the flour. Beat again until well blended. Pour into the dish and bake in the oven at gas mark 4, 180°C (350°F) for 40 minutes – the top will puff up like a soufflé. Sprinkle with icing sugar before serving.

2ⁿᵈ December

PINEAPPLE FRITTERS
Makes approx 8

1 pineapple cut into rounds, peeled and centres removed
1 tbsp caster sugar
100g, 4oz plain flour
150ml, ¼pt milk
1 egg

Sprinkle the pineapple rings with the sugar. Make up the batter by sifting the flour into a basin. Make a well in the centre and pour in the milk and egg. Mix until smooth. Dip the pineapple rings in the batter and fry for a few minutes on each side.

3rd December

BLACK TREACLE PUDDING
Serves 6

100g, 4oz butter
100g, 4oz caster sugar
2 eggs
8 tbsp black treacle
4 tbsp milk
225g, 8oz self-raising flour

Beat the butter and sugar together. Beat in the eggs and then the black treacle and milk, alternately with the flour. When everything is well combined spoon into a greased 1 litre, 2pt pudding basin, cover with greaseproof paper and secure with a rubber band. Steam for an hour. Turn out and serve with cream.

4th December

SPICY DRIED FRUIT COMPOTE
Serves 4 - 6

100g, 4oz each dried figs, apricots and prunes
50g, 2oz each of raisins, sultanas and currants
1 tsp mixed spice
3 tbsp brandy
150ml, ¼pt strong black coffee
150ml, ¼pt water

Place all the ingredients in a saucepan and bring to the boil. Simmer for 5 minutes and then transfer to a large bowl and allow to cool Chill before serving.

5ᵗʰ December

Lingonberries come originally from Sweden - the Arctic cranberry - they are a luscious red. You can buy jars of lingonberry sauce from good supermarkets or delicatessens.

LINGONBERRY AND APPLE TART
Serves 6 - 8

Pastry
225g, 8oz plain flour
100g, 4oz butter
1 egg yolk
a little water

225g, 8oz cooking apples, peeled, cored and chopped
4 tbsp lingonberry sauce
grated rind of ½ a lemon + 3 tbsp lemon juice
25g, 1oz Brazil nuts, chopped
75g, 3oz brown sugar
175g, 6oz raisins
¼ tsp ground cinnamon
¼ tsp ground nutmeg
¼ tsp ground ginger

To make the pastry, rub the butter into the flour. Bind with the egg yolk and sufficient water to make a firm dough. Knead lightly and then roll out three quarters of the pastry and line a greased 23cm, 9in flan tin. Cook the apples for 5 minutes in a little water. Mix the apples with the lingonberry sauce and add the lemon rind, lemon juice, Brazil nuts, brown sugar, raisins and spices. Stir well and fill the pastry case with this mixture. Roll out the remaining pastry and cut into strips. Cover the flan with a lattice design. Bake in the oven at gas mark 4, 180°C (350°F) for 35 minutes. Serve hot.

6ᵗʰ December

For children in Germany the highlight of Advent is St Nicholas's Day on 6ᵗʰ December. Originally children left hay and straw for St Nicholas's horses but now they simply put a shoe or boot outside their bedroom door, window or by the fireplace on the evening of 5ᵗʰ December, hoping to find it full of sweets, biscuits, nuts and fruit the next morning. Lebkuchen are traditionally eaten on this day.

LEBKUCHEN
Makes about 30 biscuits

225g, 8oz ground almonds
25g, 1oz candied peel
1tsp ground cinnamon
1 tsp ground cloves
1 tsp ground cardamom
3 eggs, separated
225g, 8oz caster sugar

Icing
grated rind of ½ a lemon
175g, 6oz icing sugar
60ml, 2fl oz boiling water

Mix together the ground almonds, candied peel and spices. Beat together the egg yolks and sugar. Beat the egg whites separately and gently fold into the egg yolk mixture. Gently fold in the ground almond mixture. Place spoonfuls on greased baking trays and bake in the oven at gas mark 4, 180°C (350°F) for 15 minutes or until they are light brown. For the icing mix the grated lemon peel into the icing sugar and gradually add the water. Beat until smooth and then spread a little icing on each biscuit.

7ᵗʰ December

This is All Saints Day in Italy. Why not celebrate with an Italian pudding - Zuccotto? There is some argument over the origin of the word. Some say it refers to the amount of sugar, 'zucchero'; others believe the literal translation of the word – skullcap – refers to the finished shape of the pudding. It is also thought that it was inspired by the cupola of the duomo (cathedral) in Florence. Whatever its origins, this dome shaped dessert begins with a bowl lined with liqueur-moistened sponge cake slices which is filled with a mixture of cream, chocolate and chopped nuts before being topped with additional cake slices.

ZUCCOTTO
Serves 6 - 8

300ml, ½pt double cream
450g, 1lb plain chocolate, finely chopped
225g, 8oz sponge cake, sliced
2 tbsp Amaretto (almond flavoured liqueur)
4 egg whites
100g, 4oz granulated sugar
50g, 2oz flaked almonds, toasted
50g, 2oz hazelnuts, toasted and ground
dusting of cocoa powder and icing sugar

Heat the cream until just below boiling point. Add the chocolate and stir until melted and the mixture is smooth. Allow to cool, stirring every so often. Line a greased pudding basin with slices of cake. Sprinkle with Amaretto. Whisk together the egg whites and sugar until stiff. Add the almonds and hazelnuts to the chocolate cream and then fold in the meringue mixture. Pour into the cake-lined bowl and cover with slices of cake. Cover and allow to set. Turn out and dust with cocoa powder and icing sugar.

Use the left over egg yolks to make custard (see page 5) and serve it with tomorrow's Chocolate Meringue Pie.

8th December

RICH CHOCOLATE MERINGUE PIE
Serves 6

Shortcrust pastry (see page 5)
150ml, ¼pt milk
100g, 4oz plain chocolate
100g, 4oz brown sugar
3 tbsp plain flour
50g, 2oz butter
2 egg yolks, beaten

Meringue Topping
2 egg whites
2 tbsp icing sugar

Roll out the pastry and use to line a greased 20cm, 8in flan tin. Prick and bake blind in the oven at gas mark 4, 180°C (350°F) for 10 minutes. To make the filling put the milk and chocolate in a saucepan and heat gently until the chocolate has melted. Mix together the brown sugar, flour, butter and egg yolks. Pour on the milk and chocolate mixture and stir well. Return to the pan and bring slowly to the boil. Then simmer, stirring all the time until the mixture is thick. Pour into the baked pastry case. Beat the egg whites until stiff and beat in the icing sugar, a spoonful at a time. Spoon over the chocolate filling and bake in the oven at gas mark 2, 150°C (300°F) for 20 minutes or until the meringue is golden. Serve warm with custard made from yesterday's egg yolks.

9ᵗʰ December

APPLE AND LEMON CURD TART
Serves 5 – 6

Shortcrust pastry (see page 5)
3 eggs
175g, 6oz caster sugar
grated rind and juice of 1 large lemon
75g, 3oz butter
225g, 8oz cooking apples, peeled and grated
2 eating apples, peeled and sliced
25g, 1oz demerara sugar

Roll the dough out on a floured surface and line a greased 20cm, 8in deep flan tin. Form a lip around the edge. Beat the eggs, caster sugar, lemon rind and juice together in a large mixing bowl. Stir in the melted butter. Grate the cooking apples directly into the mixture and mix well. Spread the runny lemon mixture over the base. Level the surface with the back of a spoon and arrange the eating apple slices around the edge, overlapping. Sprinkle over the demerara sugar. Put on a preheated baking tray and bake in the oven at gas mark 4, 180°C (350°F) for about 40-50 minutes until the centre feels firm to the touch and the apples are tinged brown.

10ᵗʰ December

APPLE AND TOFFEE MERINGUE
Serves 4

50g, 2oz light muscovado sugar
1 tbsp golden syrup
50g, 2oz butter
1 tbsp cornflour
1 tbsp lemon juice
450g, 1lb peeled, cored and sliced cooking apples

2 egg whites (use 1 egg yolk tomorrow)
100g, 4oz caster sugar

Put the muscovado sugar, syrup and butter in a saucepan and heat gently until butter has melted and the sugar has dissolved. Add the cornflour to the lemon juice and stir until smooth. Add to the sauce and continue to cook until thickened. Put the sliced apples in a 1.2 litre, 2pt round baking dish and pour the butterscotch sauce over them. Bake for 10 minutes in the oven at gas mark 4, 180°C (350°F). Whisk the egg whites until stiff and whisk in the sugar, a spoonful at a time. Take the apple out of the oven and cover with the meringue mixture. Lower the oven to gas mark 2, 150°C (300°F) and cook for 30 minutes until the meringue is browned on top. Serve warm with cream.

11ᵗʰ December

CRUMBLE TOPPED MINCE PIES
Makes 12

225g, 8oz plain flour
100g, 4oz butter
3 tbsp light muscovado sugar
1 egg yolk (from yesterday)
2 tbsp flaked almonds
225g, 8oz mincemeat

Make the pastry and crumble topping by rubbing the butter into the flour until it resembles breadcrumbs. Then stir in the sugar. Reserve half for the crumble topping. Mix the other half to a smooth dough with the egg yolk and then chill in the fridge for 15 minutes. Roll out and cut out 12 circles and press into greased patty tins. Fill with mincemeat. Mix the flaked almonds into the crumble topping and divide this mixture between the 12 tarts. Press down lightly. Bake in the oven at gas mark 5, 190°C (375°F) for 20 minutes and then cool on a wire rack and sprinkle with icing sugar.

12th December

CHOCOLATE CRÈME FRAÎCHE MOUSSE
Serves 6 – 8

175g, 6oz plain chocolate
15g, ½oz butter
3 eggs, separated
200ml, 7fl oz crème fraîche
white chocolate for decoration

Melt the chocolate and butter in the microwave or over a pan of simmering water. Stir the egg yolks into the melted chocolate mixture. Add the crème fraîche and stir until smooth. Whisk the egg whites until stiff and fold into the chocolate mixture. Pour into a serving bowl and chill until set. Decorate with shavings of white chocolate.

13th December
BUTTERMILK TART
Serves 4 - 6

Sweet shortcrust pastry (see page 5)
2 eggs
2 egg yolks
300ml, ½pt buttermilk
juice and grated rind of 1 lemon
1 tsp vanilla essence
75g, 3oz light muscovado sugar
100g, 4oz butter, melted
1 tbsp plain flour
icing sugar for dusting

Whisk together the eggs, egg yolks, buttermilk, lemon juice and rind, vanilla essence, sugar, butter and flour. Pour the mixture into a saucepan and cook over a gentle heat, stirring, until the mixture thickens. Pour into the baked pastry shell and return to the oven for 30 minutes. Leave to cool and the mixture will firm up. Dust with icing sugar before serving. Make meringue biscuits (see page 204) with the 2 left over egg whites to serve with tomorrow's rice pudding.

14ᵗʰ December

CARAMEL RICE PUDDING
Serves 4 – 6

75g, 3oz pudding rice
600ml, 1pt milk
100g, 4oz granulated sugar
2 tbsp water
150ml, ¼pt whipping cream, whipped

Put the rice in a pan and add the milk. Bring to the boil and then simmer until the milk is absorbed. Put the sugar and water in a pan and heat until the sugar dissolves. Boil without stirring until the syrup turns a dark brown colour. Pour it onto the rice and stir until the caramel melts over a gentle heat. Fold in the cream and serve.

15ᵗʰ December

APPLE FRITTERS WITH GINGER BEER
Serves 3 - 4

100g, 4oz plain flour
1 egg, separated
1 tbsp sunflower oil
150ml, ¼pt ginger beer
50g, 2oz caster sugar
3 cooking apples, peeled, cored and cut into thick rings

Sift the flour, add the egg yolk and the tablespoon of oil and gradually beat in the ginger beer. Stir in the caster sugar. Beat the egg white and fold it in. Heat some oil in a frying pan and dip each apple ring in the batter before frying them, on both sides until brown and crisp. Serve hot with sugar and single cream if liked.

16th December

MISSISSIPPI MUD PIE
Serves 8

Shortcrust pastry (see page 5)
150g, 5oz butter
25g, 1oz plain chocolate
6 tbsp cocoa powder
2 tsp coffee powder
3 eggs
25g, 1oz caster sugar
2 tbsp soured cream
3 tbsp golden syrup
1 tsp vanilla essence

Line the base and sides of a greased 23cm, 9in flan tin with the pastry. Melt the butter and chocolate together and stir in the cocoa and coffee powder. Beat the eggs and sugar until thick and add the soured cream, golden syrup and vanilla essence. Stir into the chocolate and butter mixture. Pour into the pastry shell. Cook on a baking sheet at gas mark 4, 180°C (350°F) for 35 minutes. The filling will puff up, then sink and may crack a little as it cools.

17th December

PEAR AND CRANBERRY TRIFLE
Serves 4 - 6

10 sponge fingers
240ml, 8fl oz sweet white wine
6 pears, peeled, cored and sliced
225g, 8oz granulated sugar
450g, 1lb fresh cranberries

Topping
2 eggs, separated
50g, 2oz caster sugar

225g, 8oz mascarpone
1 tbsp brandy

Layer the sponge fingers on the bottom of a serving bowl. Pour the wine over them. Poach the pears in a syrup of 4 tablespoons of water and 100g, 4oz of the granulated sugar for 15 minutes. Cook the cranberries in a small saucepan with a splash of water and the remaining sugar, bringing them up to a simmer for 10 minutes. Lay the pears on the sponge finger base and cover with the cranberries. Whisk the egg yolks with the caster sugar until thick and creamy. Beat in the mascarpone and brandy. Lastly whisk the egg whites until stiff and fold them in. Top the trifle with this mixture and chill.

18th December

Bananas were first transported to Britain in substantial quantities by Elders and Fyffes (as the company was known then) in 1901 when the first refrigerated ship, Port Morant, brought them from Jamaica. The Fruit Trade News reported in December of that year that 'bananas could be seen all day wending their way to Covent Garden'.

FLAMBÉED BANANAS
Serves 4

50g, 2oz butter
4 bananas, peeled
1 tsp lemon juice
50g, 2oz dark brown sugar
2 tbsp brandy

Heat the butter in a frying pan. Slit the bananas lengthways and sauté in the butter for 2 or 3 minutes. Sprinkle on the lemon juice and the brown sugar and continue to cook until the bananas are soft and caramelised. Pour the brandy over the bananas. If you cook on gas tilt the pan towards the flame and the juices should ignite. Otherwise light the juices with a match. The flames will die down after about 15 seconds – this takes the acidity out of the alcohol. Serve immediately.

19th December

PEAR AND CHESTNUT FLAN
Serves 4 - 6

Shortcrust pastry (see page 5)
225g, 8oz chestnut purée, sweetened
4 pears, peeled, cored and halved
4 tbsp apple jelly
25g, 1oz flaked almonds

Roll out the pastry and use to line a greased 23cm, 9in flan case. Prick the base and bake blind in the oven at gas mark 5, 190°C (375°F) for 20 minutes. Allow to cool before spreading the chestnut purée over the base of the flan. Arrange the pear halves over the purée. Heat the apple jelly gently in a small saucepan and then spread over the pears to form a glaze. To decorate, sprinkle with flaked almonds.

20th December

Save the egg yolks for tomorrow's Chocolate Bread and Butter Pudding.

CLEMENTINE MOUSSE
Serves 4

grated rind and juice of 1 orange
grated rind of 1 lime
2 tbsp caster sugar
2 tsp grated root ginger
4 clementines, peeled and segmented with pith removed
450g, 1lb cream cheese
4 egg whites

Put the grated rind and juice of the orange in a saucepan with the grated lime rind. Add the sugar and ginger. Bring to the boil and cook for 5 minutes to reduce. Pour half of the syrup over the clementine segments and leave to chill for an hour. Combine the other half of syrup with the cream cheese and whisk together. Beat egg whites until stiff and fold into the cream cheese mixture, then chill for an hour. Pour into a serving bowl and top with the clementines and syrup.

21st December

This is St Thomas's Day, when in times gone by, poor people would knock on the doors of richer households in the district to beg for flour to make bread and cakes for Christmas. Why not make a bread and butter pudding? This is a much more extravagant version than would have been possible in the past.

CHOCOLATE BREAD AND BUTTER PUDDING
Serves 8

350g, 12oz plain chocolate
600ml, 1pt single cream
600ml, 1pt milk
1 x 400g, 1lb brioche loaf
50g, 2oz butter
2 large eggs + 4 egg yolks (saved from yesterday)
200g, 7oz caster sugar
1 tsp vanilla essence

Warm the cream and milk and stir in the chocolate. Gently heat the mixture until the chocolate has all melted into the milk. Slice the brioche loaf, butter the slices and cut into triangles. Arrange in layers in an ovenproof dish. Whisk together the eggs, yolks, caster sugar and vanilla. Add the chocolate liquid and whisk until smooth. Pour over the bread. Leave for half an hour to let the bread soak up the liquid. Place the dish in a roasting tin half filled with water and bake in the oven at gas mark 4, 180°C (350°F) for 30 minutes. Serve with whipped cream.

22ⁿᵈ December

CRANBERRY FRANGIPANE TART
Serves 6

Sweet shortcrust pastry (see page 5)
225g, 8oz cranberries
100g, 4oz granulated sugar
150ml, ¼pt water

Topping
100g, 4oz butter
100g, 4oz caster sugar
2 eggs
100g, 4oz ground almonds

Roll out the pastry and use to line a greased 20cm, 8in flan case. Combine the cranberries, sugar and water. Bring to the boil and then cover and simmer for about 10 minutes. As you leave the cranberries to cool the mixture will thicken. Spread over the pastry base. For the topping cream together the butter and sugar. Stir in the eggs and ground almonds and when well amalgamated spread over the jam. Bake in the oven at gas mark 4, 180°C (350°F) for 30 minutes. Serve warm with single cream.

23rd December

CHRISTMAS APPLE PUDDING
Serves 6

100g, 4oz butter, melted
100g, 4oz light brown sugar
1 egg, beaten
100g, 4oz wholemeal flour
25g, 1oz walnuts, finely chopped
225g, 8oz cored, peeled and sliced apples, cooked with
a little water
50g, 2oz dates, chopped
½ tsp ground cinnamon
½ tsp mixed spice

Maple syrup sauce
75g, 3oz butter
6 tbsp maple syrup
150ml, ¼pt whipping cream

Mix the melted butter and sugar together. Mix in the egg and work in the flour and walnuts. Mix together the apple, dates and spices and stir into the cake mixture. Spoon into a greased 18cm, 7in square tin and bake in the oven at gas mark 4, 180°C (350°F) for 25 minutes. To make the sauce, melt the butter and syrup and stir in the cream. Boil for 5 minutes – it will become the colour of butterscotch. Serve the pudding with the sauce.

24ᵗʰ December

'Yule Logs' are a familiar part of Christmas and are associated with the ancient rites of the Norse Yule sun festival. Candles and logs are symbolic of the sun festival and of the fire and light that emanates from the sun, whilst also indicating thanks for the gifts given by the sun all year round. After the shortest day on 21ˢᵗ December, the festival looks forward to the rebirth of the sun. The Bûche de Nöel, a cake rolled and filled with chestnut cream and coated in marzipan is the French version of a Yule Log. These cakes were created in the late 19ᵗʰ century by Parisian pastry chefs who were inspired by the burning of yule logs throughout the night before Christmas.

CHOCOLATE YULE LOG
Serves 6 – 8

3 eggs
100g, 4oz caster sugar
1 tbsp hot water
50g, 2oz plain flour
25g, 1oz cocoa powder

For the filling and icing
75g, 3oz butter
3 tbsp milk
2 tbsp cocoa
300g, 10oz icing sugar

Whisk together the eggs and caster sugar until pale and thick. Stir in the hot water. Sieve the flour and cocoa powder over the egg mixture and fold it in quickly but carefully. Turn into a Swiss roll tin lined with greaseproof paper and bake in the oven at gas mark 6, 200°C (400°F) for 10 minutes. Turn out onto a piece of greaseproof paper with caster sugar sprinkled over it. Remove the lining paper and carefully roll up with the greaseproof paper inside. Allow to cool. To make the fudge icing, place the butter, milk and cocoa in a saucepan and heat gently until melted. Add the icing sugar and beat until smooth. Unroll the Swiss roll and remove the greaseproof paper.

Spread half the fudge icing over the chocolate sponge before rolling up again. Cut a short diagonal wedge off one end of the roll and join to the side of the log with some of the icing so that it resembles a branch. Spread the rest of the icing over the log and mark lines with a fork so that it looks like bark. Sprinkle with a little icing sugar.

25ᵗʰ December

CHRISTMAS PUDDING
Makes one 1.5kg, 3lb pudding

150g, 5oz self-raising flour
½ tsp ground nutmeg + 1 tsp mixed spice
25g, 1oz ground almonds
100g, 4oz shredded suet
100g, 4oz dark muscovado sugar
50g, 2oz white breadcrumbs
675g,1½lb mixed currants, raisins and sultanas
½ tbsp black treacle
grated rind and juice of ½ a lemon and ½ an orange
1 small carrot + 1 apple, peeled and grated
1 tbsp brandy, plus extra for flaming
75ml, 2½fl oz dark ale or stout
2 eggs, beaten

Sift together the flour and spices in a large bowl. Stir in the almonds, suet, sugar and breadcrumbs, mixing well. Add the remaining pudding ingredients stirring everything together. Cover with cling film and leave in the fridge for 24 hours, stirring every so often. Spoon into a 1.2 litre, 2 pint pudding basin. Top the surface of the pudding with a circle of greaseproof paper, then cover with more greaseproof paper and secure with a rubber band. Steam for about 6 hours, topping up with water every so often. Leave to cool, removing the greaseproof paper and replace it with another piece. The pudding should be stored in a cool, dry place. On Christmas morning steam the pudding for a further two hours. Heat a little brandy in a small saucepan and carefully touch a lighted match to the edge of the saucepan. When ready to serve, turn out the pudding and pour the flaming alcohol onto it.

26th December

St Stephen's Day is known almost universally as Boxing Day. In Christian tradition an offering box was placed in the church, which remained unopened all year round. The box was opened on Christmas Day, and the contents distributed by the priests. The contents were called the 'dole of the Christmas box' or 'box money'. Before the introduction of the Christmas Pudding came the Mince Pie in the mid-1500s. It has been traditional to eat a pie each day for the Twelve Days of Christmas. This was said to ensure that the following twelve months would be happy. In the South of England it was thought best to eat each pie in a different house. The first Mince Pies were oblong in shape and known to have been made in Roman times. In Christian times the shape of the pie was said to reflect the shape of Christ's cradle, and had no pastry top.

MINCE PIES
Makes 12

150g, 5oz plain flour
75g, 3oz butter
25g, 1oz icing sugar
grated rind of ½ a lemon
1 egg, separated
1 tbsp milk
175g, 6oz mincemeat

To make the pastry rub the butter into the flour. Sift in the icing sugar and add the grated lemon rind. Mix together the egg yolk and milk and stir into the dry ingredients. Bind together and knead lightly until smooth. Leave to cool for 30 minutes and then roll out and stamp out 24 circles. Grease a 12-hole patty tin and press circles into the compartments. Put a teaspoonful of mincemeat into each pastry case. Top with the 12 left over circles and press down. Brush with a little beaten egg white and bake in the oven at gas mark 5, 190°C (375°F) for about 20 minutes. Mince pies will keep for about two weeks in an airtight tin. If liked serve with this delicious brandy butter ice cream.

BRANDY BUTTER ICE CREAM
Serves 4 - 6

300ml, ½pt double cream
150ml, ¼pt milk
150g, 5oz icing sugar
1 tbsp vanilla essence
5 tbsp brandy
75g, 3oz unsalted butter, softened

Beat the double cream and milk together. Stir in the icing sugar, vanilla essence, brandy and butter. Spoon into a freezer container and freeze until firm.

27ᵗʰ December

This is a comforting but light pudding, originally from the US, and a possible alternative to Christmas pudding. If you have bought cranberries to make cranberry sauce you may have some left over.

PILGRIM'S PUDDING
Serves 6 – 8

225g, 8oz cranberries, chopped
75g, 3oz butter, diced
50g, 2oz demerara sugar
2 tsp mixed spice
225g, 8oz self-raising flour
175g, 6oz black treacle, warmed
5 tbsp milk
1 tsp vanilla essence

Put half the pieces of butter and a quarter of the cranberries in the bottom of a greased 1.75litre, 3pint pudding basin. Sprinkle half the demerara sugar and half the mixed spice over the top. Rub the rest of the butter into the flour and mix in the rest of the cranberries. Mix the black treacle with the milk and vanilla essence and stir into the flour mixture. Spoon into the basin. Sprinkle the rest of the demerara sugar and mixed spice over the top. Seal as for a steamed pudding and steam for 2 hours. Serve with butterscotch sauce (see page 121).

28ᵗʰ December

CHOCOLATE MARQUISE
Serves 4 - 6

175g, 6oz plain chocolate
100g, 4oz white chocolate
2 tbsp single cream
75g, 3oz butter
100g, 4oz caster sugar
3 egg yolks
1 tbsp brandy
300ml, ½pt double cream

Melt the two chocolates separately and stir the single cream into the white chocolate. Beat together the butter with half the caster sugar and mix half into the plain chocolate and half into the white chocolate. Beat the egg yolks with the rest of the caster sugar and again divide between the two chocolates. Stir the brandy into the plain chocolate mixture. Whip the cream and fold into each chocolate mixture. Put alternate spoonfuls into a pudding basin or mould and then swirl together to give a marbled effect. Smooth the top. Chill for a few hours before turning out. Make a batch of meringues (page 6) or meringue biscuits (page 204) with left over egg whites.

29ᵗʰ December

MARMALADE PUDDING
Serves 4 - 6

3 tbsp marmalade
175g, 6oz self-raising flour
75g, 3oz softened butter
50g, 2oz caster sugar
1 egg
6 tbsp milk

Grease a 1.2 litre, 2pt pudding basin and spoon the marmalade into the bottom of it. Mix together the flour, butter and sugar. Make a well in the centre and beat in the egg and enough milk to give a good dropping consistency. Spoon over the marmalade and cover with greaseproof paper, secured with a rubber band. Steam for 1½ hours. Turn out and serve with cream.

30ᵗʰ December

COFFEE YULE LOG
Serves 8

2 eggs
1 egg yolk
75g, 3oz caster sugar
50g, 2oz plain flour
1 tbsp cornflour
1 tbsp coffee essence

Filling
150ml, ¼pt double cream
25g, 1oz icing sugar
1 tbsp coffee essence

Whisk together the eggs, egg yolk and caster sugar until thick and creamy. Sift together the flour and cornflour and gently fold into the egg mixture along with the coffee essence. Turn into a Swiss roll tin, lined with greaseproof paper and bake in the oven at gas mark 6, 200°C (400°F) for 10 minutes or until springy to the touch. Lay a piece of greaseproof paper on your work surface and sprinkle caster sugar over it. Turn the sponge out carefully, remove the lining paper and roll up with the greaseproof paper inside. Allow to cool while you whip the cream with the icing sugar and coffee essence. Unroll, remove this greaseproof paper and spread the coffee cream over the sponge before rolling up again. Sprinkle with icing sugar before serving.

31st December

Celebrate New Year's Eve with a deliciously moreish pudding.

STICKY TOFFEE PUDDING
Serves 6

50g, 2oz butter
75g, 3oz caster sugar
2 eggs
100g, 4oz dates, chopped
90ml, 3fl oz water
90ml, 3fl oz evaporated milk
1 tsp bicarbonate of soda
1 tbsp coffee essence
100g, 4oz self-raising flour

Toffee Sauce
50g, 2oz butter
75g, 3oz brown sugar
90ml, 3fl oz double cream

Beat together the butter and sugar. Gradually beat in the eggs. Heat the dates in the water and evaporated milk and simmer for a few minutes. Add the bicarbonate of soda. The mixture will froth a little. Allow to cool slightly and then mix into the butter mixture together with the coffee essence and flour. Stir until smooth. Pour into a greased baking dish and cook for 25 minutes in the oven at gas mark 4, 180°C (350°F). To make the toffee sauce melt the butter and sugar together and stir in the cream. Cook for 3 or 4 minutes stirring until the sauce has thickened slightly. Serve the pudding with the toffee sauce and cream if liked.

Index

A

Angel's Food Cake 112
Apple & Blackberry Hot Soufflés 160
Apple & Blackberry Crumble 184
Apple & Blackcurrant Ice Cream 181
Apple & Blueberry Walnut Crisp 170
Apple & Cardamom Crumble 196
Apple & Date Brown Betty 215
Apple & Fig Crumble 188
Apple & Gingerbread Trifle 211
Apple & Grape Pie 216
Apple & Lemon Curd Tart 234
Apple & Lemon Tartlets 197
Apple & Toffee Meringue 234
Apple Butterscotch Meringue Pie 185
Apple Charlotte 168
Apple Cobbler 182
Apple Cake, Danish 18
Apple Cake, Somerset 196
Apple Flapjack Pudding 204
Apple Fritters 188
Apple Fritters With Ginger Beer 237
Apple Fudge Pudding 199
Apple Pie 193
Apple Slump 226
Apple Turnovers 191
Apricot & Almond Tart 161
Apricot Ice Cream 155
Autumn Pudding 180
Avocado And Lime Whip 53

B

Baked Alaska 162
Baked Peaches with Raspberries 133
Bakewell Pudding 31
Baklava 64
Banana & Honey Ice Cream 32
Banana Fritters 42

Barnstaple Fair Pears 176
Bavarian Strudel 178
Black Treacle Delight 9
Black Treacle Pudding 229
Blackberry & Apple Amber 172
Blackberry Ice Cream 175
Blackberry Snow 166
Blackcurrant & Apple Crumble 158
Blackcurrant & Chocolate Trifle 136
Blackcurrant & Lime Sorbet 147
Blackcurrant & Ricotta Dessert 122
Blackcurrant Clafoutis 132
Blackcurrant Leaf Water Ice 110
Blackcurrant Sponge Pudding 126
Blueberry & Nectarine Cobbler 150
Blueberry & Vanilla Pavlova 137
Blueberry Cheesecake 140
Blueberry Frangipane Tart 146
Blueberry Ice Cream 135
Blueberry Pie 143
Bramble Mousse 168
Brandy Butter Ice Cream 247
Brazil Nut Cake 80
Bread & Butter Pudding 145
Brown Sugar & Cream Ambrosia 13
Brown Sugar Meringues 35
Buttermilk Tart 236
Butterscotch Ice Cream 60
Butterscotch Pudding 177
Butterscotch Tart 38

C

Caledonian Cream 227
Cape Gooseberry & Pear Crumble 195
Caramel & Crushed Meringue with
    Strawberries 111
Caramel Apple & Date Muffin Cake
    201
Caramel Cheesecake 219
Caramel Rice Pudding 237
Caramel Steamed Pudding 214
Caramelised Apple Sponge 207
Carrot & Apple Tart 202

Cattern Pie 223
Champagne Fruit Salad 72
Charlotte Malakoff 109
Cheesecake
Blueberry 140, Caramel 219,
Chestnut 16, Chocolate &
Brandy 37, Easy Chocolate 224,
Gooseberry 106, Guava 51, Irish
Coffee 54, Marbled Chocolate 77,
Strawberry Lemon 110
Cherry & Almond Tart 93
Cherry & Redcurrant Upside Down Cake
152
Cherry Clafoutis 166
Cherry Compote 95
Cherry Soufflé Omelette 91
Chestnut Charlotte 202
Chestnut Cheesecake 16
Chestnut Soufflé 69
Chestnut Tiramisu 40
Chestnut Trifle 27
Chocolate & Brandy Cheesecake 37
Chocolate & Chestnut Ice Cream 213
Chocolate & Hazelnut Pudding 187
Chocolate & Lemon Mousse 78
Chocolate & Pear Meringue Pie 174
Chocolate & Walnut Ice Cream Cake 43
Chocolate Bakewell Tart 20
Chocolate Bread & Butter Pudding 241
Chocolate Brownie Tarts 48
Chocolate Caramel Tart 70
Chocolate Crème Fraîche Mousse 236
Chocolate Fondue 18
Chocolate Fudge Ice Cream 44
Chocolate Ice Cream 116
Chocolate Marquise 248
Chocolate Melting Puddings 14
Chocolate Meringue Roulade 216
Chocolate Mousse Cake 48
Chocolate Pancakes with Cream 52
Chocolate, Pear & Raspberry Upside
Down Pudding 200

Chocolate Pecan Tart 19
Chocolate Pots 157
Chocolate Profiteroles with Coffee
Cream And Chocolate Sauce 58
Chocolate Rice Pudding 191
Chocolate Roulade 50
Chocolate Sauce 59, 200
Chocolate Soufflé 40
Chocolate Surprise Pudding 55
Chocolate Syrup Tart 97
Chocolate Truffles 35
Chocolate Yule Log 244
Christmas Apple Pudding 243
Christmas Pudding 223, 245
Cider Cake 17
Clafoutis
Blackcurrant 132, Cherry 166,
Mulberry 147, Nectarine 114
Clementine Mousse 240
Coeurs a la Creme 34
Coffee Pancakes with Chocolate Fudge
Sauce 39
Coffee Sorbet with White Chocolate
Sauce 129
Coffee Yule Log 249
Cranberry Frangipane Tart 242
Cream Cheese & Pineapple Paskha 83
Cream Crowdie 22
Crema Catalana 56
Crème Brulée 63
Crème Caramel 47
Crepes Suzette 36
Crumble Topped Mince Pies 235

D
Damson Syllabub 190
Danish Apple Cake 18
Date, Walnut & Fig Tart 180
Devil's Food Cake 104
Double Chocolate Terrine 198
Dulce de Leche Cake 192

E

Easy Chocolate Cheesecake 224
Easy Creamy Flan 95
Easy Lemon Mousse 88
Elderflower Fritters 105
Epiphany Tart 10
Eton Mess 106
Eve's Pudding 190

F

Figgy Pudding 62
Flambeed Bananas 239
Floating Island - Ile Flottante 42
Fool
   Mango with Blueberries 30,
   Marbled Rhubarb 66, Persimmon
   25, Plum & Bramble 174
Frangipane
   Blueberry Tart 146, Cranberry Tart
   242, Pineapple Tart 108
Fritters
   Apple 188, Apple with Ginger
   Beer 237, Banana 42, Elderflower
   105, Pineapple 228
Fruit Savarin 117
Fudge & Chocolate Cream Tart 217

G

Galician Almond Tart 139
Gateau St Honore 94
Gin & Lavender Ice Cream 92
Ginger Biscuit Pudding 24
Gold & Silver Cakes 86
Golden Apple Pudding 131
Golden Syrup Bread Pudding 74
Gooseberry & Elderflower Fool 103
Gooseberry Cheesecake 106
Granary Bread Ice Cream 84
Grape & Cream Cheese Flan 89
Grape & Honey Whip 76
Greengage Tart 164
Guards Pudding 221

Guava Cheesecake 51
Gulab Jamun 154

H

Hazelnut Ice Cream 215
Hazelnut Roulade 101
Heg Peg Dump 135
Honeycomb Ice Cream 74
Hot Apple Meringue Trifle 10

I

Iced Peach Soufflé 119
Iced Redcurrant Meringue 139
Irish Coffee Cheesecake 54

J

Jam Roly Poly Pudding 19

K

Kent Lent Pie 49
Kiwi Fruit Sorbet 69
Kiwi Fruit Syllabub 75

L

Lady Stanhope's Baalbek Apples 51
Lebkuchen 231
Lemon & Blackcurrant Surprise
   Pudding 142
Lemon & Elderflower Syllabub 107
Lemon & Fromage Frais Mousse 16
Lemon & Hazelnut Roulade 212
Lemon & Lime Ice Cream 85
Lemon & Lime Soufflé 67
Lemon & Lime Syllabub 100
Lemon Caramel Cream 118
Lemon Curd & Almond Tart 71
Lemon Curd Ice Cream 90
Lemon Fudge Tart 102
Lemon Geranium Sorbet 112
Lemon Kiwi Slices 82
Lemon Meringue Pie 28

Lemon Meringue Roulade with
Blueberries 38
Lemon Rice Pudding 204
Lemon Sorbet 48
Lemon Surprise Pudding 97
Lemon Syllabub 116
Lemon Syrup Tart 222
Lemon Tart with Chocolate Ginger Crust
    15
Lime Tart 82
Lingonberry & Apple Tart 230
Log Fire Gingerbread Pudding 209
Loganberry Meringue Ice Cream
    Pudding 152
Loganberry Snow 155
Loganberry Water Ice 163

M

Macadamia Toffee Tart 24
Manchester Tart 99
Mango Fool with Blueberries 30
Mango Mousse 14
Maple & Walnut Praline Ice Cream 183
Maple Syrup & Apple Sponge 194
Maple Syrup & Pecan Pie 60
Maple Syrup Ice Cream 67
Maple Syrup Nutty Cake 212
Marbled Chocolate Cheesecake 77
Marbled Rhubarb Fool 66
Marmalade Pudding 248
Mascarpone Ice Cream 127
Melon & Peach Sorbet 148
Melon Ice Cream 120
Meringues 6
    Brown Sugar 35, Muscovado 92
Meringue Biscuits 204
Mince Pies 246
Mini Autumn Puddings 218
Mini Coffee Caramel Puddings 30
Mini Pumpkin & Ginger Puddings 206
Mint & Blackcurrant Mousse 134
Mint Ice Cream 86
Mint, Lime & Melon Sorbet 109

Mississippi Mud Pie 238
Mocha Cream Cheese Pie 88
Mocha Layered Creamy Pudding 25
Molasses Ice Cream 57
Mont Blanc 221
Mousse
    Bramble 168, Chocolate and Lemon
    78, Chocolate Creme Fraiche 236,
    Clementine 240, Easy Lemon 88,
    Lemon & Fromage Frais 16,
    Mango 14, Mint & Blackcurrant 134,
    Raspberry & Redcurrant 145, St
    Clement's 65, Strawberry 118, White
    Chocolate 111
Mulberrry Pie 164
Mulberry & Pear Upside Down Pudding
    169
Mulberry Clafoutis 147
Muscovado Meringues with Passion Fruit
    & Mascarpone 92

N

Nectarine Clafoutis 114
Norfolk Treacle Tart 32

O

Oeufs a la Neige 218
Orange Ice Cream 33
Orange Trifle 45
Oranges, Caramelised 8
Ozark Pudding 124

P

Pancake batter 6
Pancakes, Chocolate with Cream 38
Pancakes, Coffee 39
Pancakes with Lemon & Sugar 33
Pancakes with Special Lemon Sauce 61
Papaya & Pomegranate Pavlova 56
Paris-Brest 167
Parkin 211
Paskha 68
Passion Fruit Ice Cream 59

Pavlova
 Pineapple & Kiwi 22, Papaya &
 Pomegranate 56, Blueberry & Vanilla
 137, Pear and Raspberry 128
Peach & Blackcurrant Summer Pie 157
Peach & Hazelnut Ice Cream 189
Peach & Walnut Upside Down Pudding
 96
Peaches in Butterscotch Sauce 28
Peaches with Elderflower-flavoured
 Strawberries 114
Pear & Blackberry Sponge Pudding 179
Pear & Blackcurrant Streusel Pie 124
Pear & Chestnut Flan 240
Pear & Cranberry Trifle 238
Pear & Raspberry Pavlova 128
Pear & Redcurrant Cobbler 171
Pears Belle Hélène 163
Pears with Redcurrant Sorbet 165
Persimmon Fool 25
Pilgrim's Pudding 247
Pineapple & Blueberry Upside Down
 Pudding 11
Pineapple & Kiwi Pavlova 22
Pineapple Caramel Cream 29
Pineapple Frangipane Tart 108
Pineapple Fritters 228
Pineapple Sorbet 20
Plum & Bramble Fool 174
Plum & Port Parfait 173
Plum Pudding 102
Poached Pears with Strawberries 105
Poppy Seed & Lemon Cake 46
Primrose Gateau 78
Profiteroles with Butterscotch Sauce 121
Prune souffle 214
Pumpkin Cake 203
Pumpkin Pie 224

Q

Queen of Puddings 79
Quince & Ginger Crumble 205

R

Raspberry & Chocolate Cream Pudding
 130
Raspberry Cream Ice with Redcurrant
 Ripple 160
Raspberry & Redcurrant Mousse 145
Raspberry & Watermelon Cream Ice 125
Raspberry Ice Cream 128
Raspberry Sorbet 172
Red Berry Jelly 123
Redcurrant & Honey Ice Cream 158
Redcurrant Bavarois 156
Rhubarb & Apple Charlotte 58
Rhubarb & Banana Pudding 93
Rhubarb Brown Betty 85
Rhubarb Crumble 89
Rhubarb Yoghurt Ice 96
Rice Pudding with Raspberry Sauce 150
Rich Caramel Ice Cream 76
Rich Chocolate Meringue Pie 233
Rich Chocolate Steamed Pudding 12
Ripe Tart 148
Rodgrod Med Flode 141
Romanian Cheese Soufflé 228
Roulade
 Chocolate 50, Hazelnut 101,
 Lemon & Hazelnut 212

S

Saint Emilion au Chocolat 130
Sand Cake with Raspberries 81
Scottish Flummery 126
Semi Freddo Banana Cream 205
Shoo Fly Pie 225
Shortcrust Pastry 5
Sicilian Cassata 70
Somerset Apple Cake 196
Sorbet
 Blackcurrant & Lime 147, Coffee129,
 Lemon 48, Lemon Geranium 112,
 Kiwi Fruit 75, Mint, Lime & Melon
 109, Pineapple 20, Raspberry 172,

Redcurrant 165 Summer
Fruits 156
Soufflé
  Cherry 91, Chestnut 69,
  Chocolate 40, Lemon & Lime
  67, Prune 214, Romanian
  Cheese 228
Soul Cakes 208
Soured Cream Raisin & Pecan Pie
  122
Spicy Dried Fruit Compote 229
Sponge & Chocolate Upside
  Down Pudding 220
Spotted Dick 54
St Clement's Mousse 65
Steamed Lemon Sponge Pudding
  8
Sticky Caramel Tart 107
Sticky Toffee Pudding 250
Strawberry & Lemon Tipsy Trifle
  115
Strawberry Ice Cream 113
Strawberry Lemon Cheesecake
  110
Strawberry Mousse 118
Summer Fruits Sorbet 157
Summer Pudding with Nectarines
  151
Sussex Pond Pudding 27
Syllabub
  Damson 191, Kiwi Fruit 69,
  Lemon 111, Lemon &
  Elderflower 107, Lemon &
  Lime 100

T

Tarte Tatin 186
Tayberry & Amaretto Trifle 162
Tayberry & Chocolate Tartlets 149
Tayberry & Nectarine Toffee
  Puddings 153
Texas Osgood Pecan Pie 222

Tiramisu 100
Toffee Apples 159
Toffee Ice Cream 111
Toffee Pastries 121
Toffee Tart with Brazil Nut Pastry 87
Toffee Walnut Tart 182
Traditional Summer Pudding 132
Treacle Pudding 210
Treacle Tart 46
Trifle
  Apple & Gingerbread 211,
  Blackcurrant & Chocolate 136,
  Hot Apple Meringue 11, Orange
  45, Pear & Cranberry 238,
  Strawberry & Lemon Tipsy 115,
  Tayberry & Amaretto 163, Typsy
  Laird - Scots Trifle 23
Tropical Fruit Salad 34
Truffle Torte 73
Twelfth Night Cake 9
Typsy Laird - Scots Trifle 23

V

Vanilla Custard Tart 13
Vanilla Ice Cream with Blackcurrant
  Kissel 144
Vasilopita 7
Velvety Chocolate Cream 52

W

Walnut & Apple Tart 184
Walnut Lemon Meringue 84
Walnut Treacle Tart 91
Welsh Amber Pudding 45
White Chocolate Heavens 21
White Chocolate Mousse 111

Z

Zabaglione 41
Zabaglione Ice Cream 138
Zuccotto 232